Pub Walks in the Lake District

Neil Coates

Published by Sigma Leisure – an imprint of
Sigma Press, 1 South Oak Lane, Wilmslow, Cheshire SK9 6AR, England.

Whilst every effort has been made to ensure that the information given in this book is correct, neither the publisher nor the author accept any responsibility for any inaccuracy.

British Library Cataloguing in Publication Data
A CIP record for this book is available from the British Library.

First printed in 1992
Reprinted 1993 (twice)

ISBN: 1-85058-293-9

Typesetting and Design by: Sigma Press, Wilmslow, Cheshire

Maps by: Pam Upchurch

Cover photograph: The Britannia Inn, Elterwater (photograph by David Fry)

Text photographs: taken by the author, except for those on pages 18, 77, 128, 137 and 144, which are by Graham Beech.

Printed by: Manchester Free Press

Preface

Hardly a week goes by, it seems, without another book concerning the Lake District appearing on the bookshelves. So why add this volume to the fray? In short, it's unique.

Whilst Wainwright, Poucher *et al.* have documented, drawn and photographed every nook, cranny, stile, peak and tarn in the region they only make passing reference to that most traditional and necessary of Lake District structures, the public house. Similarly, that dedicated group of crusaders The Campaign for Real Ale (CAMRA) have produced learned tomes celebrating the British pub and draught beer, but rarely include walks of greater distance than that from car park to pub or from bar to w.c. This book aims to help fill that yawning gap which separates, in terms of the printed word, fell walker and dipsomaniac.

These 25 walks offer the best of both worlds. Each is based on a tavern purveying some of the finest draught beer to be found, and describes in detail a walk from into the surrounding glorious countryside. Some of the walks are "classics" which you'll find in most other guidebooks - which is how they became classics! Many of them, however, are unusual enough to make meeting more than a couple more walkers en route something to write home about. In the same vein, several of the pubs are so well known as to need little introduction whilst others are a real discovery, "worth passing a few other pubs for" as the saying goes.

The walks are grouped into three sections, based on the "traditional" English counties before local government reorganisation nearly twenty years ago: Cumberland, Westmorland and Lancashire. Today's Cumbria encompasses virtually all of the first two of these plus Lancashire-over-the-Sands, that chunk of the Lake District and South Cumbria which includes Barrow, the Dunnerdale Fells and Coniston Water, once Lancashire's largest lake. The Three Shires Stone, at the summit of the Wrynose Pass, marks the place where these three Counties once met.

Two things you won't find in this book are high level/strenuous walks - none of the walks climbs above 2000 feet and all are aimed at the casual rambler who enjoys an occasional scramble rather than the dedicated fellwalker - or walks in the western Lake District. This latter area is covered comprehensively in the Sigma Press volume "Western Lakeland Rambles - Copeland" by Gordon Brown, virtually all of the walks passing close to a pub which sells real ale.

Of the hundreds of pubs and thousands of miles of footpaths in the region I've made a personal selection that should appeal to a wide cross section. No two walks are alike, each has its own unique atmosphere, history, connections, folklore or attractions which I've detailed in the text. The pubs, too, each have their own character and idiosyncrasies, as often as not a product of the licensees who, without exception, strive to make even the most bedraggled of walkers very welcome.

From coast to cwm, mossland to mountainside, the area in and around the Lake District has a lifetime's supply of rambles and scrambles to satisfy even the most discerning of country lovers. By happy chance, a lifetime's drinking opportunities for the connoisseur of real ale and real pubs shares the same area of the map. Let *"Pub Walks in the Lake District"* help put you on the road (or footpath...) to this nirvana!

Acknowledgment: A lot of bootleather has gone into this book – not all of it mine. Similarly, a lot of glasses have been wetted. My grateful thanks go to Tim Bassett and Fred Laugharne, for their uncanny ability to spot a stile or a route through (or into) a bog despite carrying half a brewery around with them. Thanks also to Kevin Murphy, Steve Marriot, Dave Keen, Mike Pole, Glyn Broadley and Anthony M. O'Brien.

Half (at least) the fun of the research was visiting a vast number of pubs – all of them sell draught beer and all offer an enthusiastic welcome to walkers. I'm indebted to the licensees and staff I buttonholed for many a tale and anecdote about the pubs and local area.

Neil Coates

Contents

The Walks

Cumberland

Westmorland

Lancashire-over-the-Sands

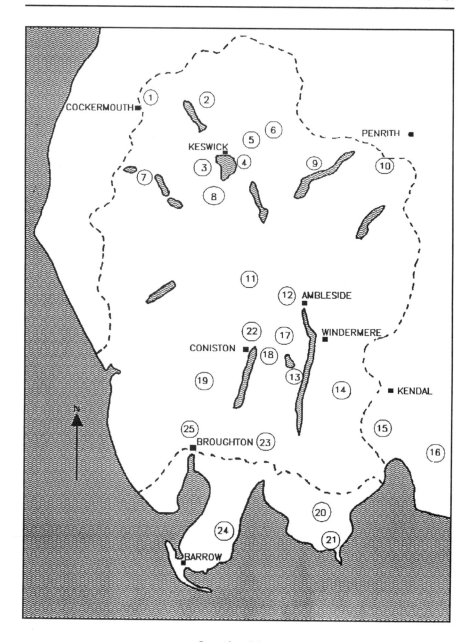

Location Map

Breweries, Beers & Pubs

In Cumbria as a whole, there remains but a small handful of working breweries. The largest is Jennings of Cockermouth, supplying their own 76 pubs plus a lot of free houses with up to four different beers – three bitters and a mild. Just down the road in Westnewton, Yates' was set up in an old farm brewery in 1986 by the former head brewer from Jennings; this tiny company now supplies a growing number of free houses with an excellent bitter which has already become a firm favourite amongst beer connoisseurs (try it at the Drunken Duck on the Barngates walk in this book) and, occasionally, an Ambrosia-like Premium Bitter.

The other large brewery in the region is Hartley's of Ulverston. They supply three bitters and a mild to around 60 tied houses, mostly in the south of Cumbria. Sadly, the distinctive taste of their beers looks destined to become nothing but a wistful memory as the brewery owners, regional brewers Robinson's of Stockport, plan to close the Ulverston plant and brew the beers in Stockport.

Such closures and rationalisations are nothing new to the drinkers of Cumbria. The last surviving State Brewery, in Carlisle, renowned for the modest price of its beers, was taken over in the early 1970's by Theakston's who themselves were swallowed up by Matthew Brown's of Blackburn in the mid 1980's. Now they in turn have become a part of the brewing conglomerate Scottish and Newcastle. The end result is that two breweries – at Carlisle and at Workington – have been closed in the interests of rationalisation. Other old favourites disappeared long ago, Kendal's Beezon Brewery (Jones, Alexander and Sons), for example is now a leading Arts Centre.

The news is not all bad, however. In addition to the three working breweries listed above there are three home-brew pubs whose beers are available at the brewing pub and a handful of other outlets. The three are the Sun Inn in Dent (near Sedbergh), the Masons Arms at Strawberry Bank, above Windermere, and the Old Crown at Hesket Newmarket, high in the Caldbeck Fells northeast of Skiddaw. Of these, beers from the latter can be sampled at The Mill in Mungrisdale (see the Mungrisdale walk).

Most of the pubs in and around the Lake District are owned by the three breweries, Jennings, Hartleys and Scottish and Newcastle. In virtually all of them you can get a pint or two of the real stuff, almost always from the brewery that actually owns the pub – the idea of getting in a guest beer from an outside brewery hasn't caught on in this region. As each of these breweries produces excellent beer (Scottish and Newcastle pubs invariably have Theakstons available) the discerning drinker has little to fear. In addition there is an increasing number of free houses in the area, taking beers not only from the local micro-breweries but also national favourites such as Marston's Pedigree and Bass and regional brews from the likes of Thwaite's (Blackburn) and Mitchells (Lancaster).

The pubs included in this book are obviously a personal choice. In truth the difficulty came in choosing which ones not to include. The trouble with the Lake District and environs is that it is bursting with excellent pubs, most of which are slap-bang in the midst of glorious walking opportunities. Thus some pubs which are part of everyday parlance amongst ramblers – The Old Dungeon Ghyll in Great Langdale and The Mortal Man in Troutbeck for example – are excluded simply through lack of space. The far western valleys and fells are also excluded, for the reason given in the preface. Excluded with them are classic walkers pubs such as the Wasdale Head Inn, The Woolpack at Boot and the Screes at Strands, all of which would surely otherwise have been featured.

Another favourite, The Mason's Arms at Strawberry Bank, northeast of Newby Bridge, not only brews its own beer but also sells a comprehensive series of walks leaflets based on the pub – which is the only reason why I've not included this amazing establishment in this book. Once you've completed the walks in this book try experimenting with a few others, there's a decent pub around almost every corner and at the other side of almost every ridge!

Opening Hours

This is something of an "How long is a piece of string?" poser. Being the popular tourist area it is, hours of opening tend to vary between summer and winter...but the definition of summer and winter varies from pub to pub! At the time I undertook the majority of the research for the book (summer 1991) the question of opening hours for 1992 was something to be confirmed later in the year; some were planning to open all day, some to experiment with extended lunchtime hours and some to cut back. Where possible I've included hours of opening in the text, but it's very much a case of chancing your luck at many of the pubs. In general, most of the town pubs stay open all day, 11am to 11pm whilst most of the country pubs tend to open between 11am and 3pm then 6pm to 11pm (ie the "old" hours), although there are inevitably exceptions in both camps.

Geology And Scenery

The Rocks

The bare bones that are the mountains of The Lake District reveal a geological history more complex than virtually any other part of England. A commonly used analogy is to imagine that the region is an upturned bowl. The rim of the bowl is mostly limestone (with a peripheral area of sandstone), the sides of the bowl are slates whilst the central area is dominated by volcanic rocks. The youngest rocks (the sandstones) are, perhaps, only 200 million years old, the most ancient ones date back nearly 500 million years.

This is obviously a huge over-simplification but it does help to explain the distinctive scenery that marks one part of the Lakes from another. In the north, for example, the great whaleback hills of Skiddaw and Back 'o Skiddaw, sharpened, sliced and honed by remarkably erosive streams, take their characteristic shape from the slabby slates which are the dominant rock. These originated as muds, shales and sands laid down in a shallow sea 500 million years ago, later to be forced upwards as part of the dome-like structure that is the Lake District and transformed by this pressure into the Skiddaw Slates that tower so menacingly over Keswick.

Only a handful of miles south of Keswick the scenery has a completely different character. There are still the mountains of course, but here they are craggy and angular, less affected by the erosive power of water and made up of lavas and ashes erupted from volcanoes in a far more recent age than that which saw the sea which produced the Skiddaw mother-rock. These rocks are given the collective title Borrowdale Volcanics (after the valley south of Derwent Water) and include the highest of the mountains, Scafell, Helvellyn, and the eponymous Crinkle Crags as well as those most-recognisable of peaks, The Langdale Pikes.

Travel a further few miles south again and the realm of the highest mountains is left behind. The lower, more undulating countryside around Windermere and Hawkshead, Newby Bridge and Furness result from a complex mixture of limestones, sandstones and slates far younger than the Skiddaw variety of the northern fells. Few peaks make even 1500 feet and the characteristic landforms include areas of craggy limestone and sudden, sharp scars that cut for miles across the countryside such as Scout Scar and Whitbarrow Scar between Kendal and Windermere. The areas of younger slates and associated volcanic rocks stand out as areas such as the Dunnerdale Fells, south west of Coniston and the southern end of Grizedale Forest – the Silurian Way waymarked footpath in this Forest takes its name from the geological time period during which many of the rocks were formed.

There are, of course, myriad localised geological features that go to emphasize the generality of the above. Thus Coniston Old Man and adjacent fells, certainly in the southern part of the Lakes, consist largely of volcanic rocks; Black Combe, that mysterious and lonely fell above Millom, the furthest southwest you can get, consists of Skiddaw Slates and the famous Shap Pink Granite, a volcanic rock, is quarried in the midst of the gritstones and sandstones of the Shap Fells.

The Work of Ice

That this geological skeleton plays host to those features after which the area is named – the lakes – is due to a recent player in the development and shaping of the landscape, glaciers. It's a mere ten thousand years since the last glaciers lost their fight against the warming atmosphere and melted into history, but their effect on the landscape and scenery has been profound. All of the lakes we know today formed as a result of this last great period of glaciation. The largest of all, Windermere, fills the site of a relatively shallow, meandering valley (albeit one made slightly deeper by the actions of an ice sheet) and is held back, dammed in, by a great wedge of glacial deposits – a moraine – which completely blocked the neck of the old valley, causing the waters to build up and create a lake. The "old" River Leven would once have flowed along the foot of Newton Fells and through Cartmel to reach the sea; today it flows through the deep Backbarrow Gorge and to the sea at Greenodd, a new course dictated by the effects of glacial melt water draining over the lowest part of the moraine.

In other places where now there are several lakes there once was but one. Buttermere and Crummock Water, for example, all but fill the floor of the dramatic glaciated valley gouged by a glacier which once stretched from the Honister Pass well towards the coast. Only recently has the boggy, low lying meadowland beside Buttermere village been built up by silts deposited by Sail Beck and Buttermere Dubs to form two separate sheets of water. Loweswater, northwest of Crummock Water, was undoubtedly part of the same huge post-glacial lake before it, too, was isolated by silting. The same history applies to Derwent Water and Bassenthwaite which were once a single lake, now split asunder by (relatively) recent silting.

Ullswater lies in a greatly overdeepened valley gouged out by the ice. One of the deeper lakes – over 150 feet in places – it will take a lot of silting up but the process is already well under way. Photographs of the head of the lake at Patterdale and Glenridding taken today and compared with Victorian era shots of the same spot show that the area of marshy meadowland has significantly increased. Similar new land at Sandwick and Howtown on its southern shore and Watermillock on the west suggest that in a few thousand years the lake will, inevitably, be a lot smaller than it is now. The view from Kirkstone Pass north towards Ullswater is down a splendid "U-shaped" valley gouged by a glacier, a view rivalled only by the view down the Honister Pass.

At least two lakes have already disappeared. Lonely Kentmere, east of Windermere, was once host to two shallow lakes separated by a moraine; the upper one is completely silted up whilst only tiny Kentmere Tarn remains as a shadow of the lower one and this is largely because of the digging of diatomite, a silica rich organic deposit.

The Hand of Man

Man's impact on the landscape has been largely cosmetic, but none the less dramatic for that. To the casual observer the most obvious man made features are the towns and villages, the roads and railways. Whilst such have an effect on a micro-scale – hence the furore when a new by-pass is planned, an old farm renovated in a visually unappealing style or low cost housing suggested in a National Park settlement – this is essentially an esoteric effect, detracting from the beauty of the natural landscape.

This "natural landscape" is, in fact, far from being such. Much of the beauty beloved of visitors and residents alike is a product of several thousand years' exploitation by humans. Take the bare moorlands and uplands for example. There is, dictated by nature, an altitude above which trees will not grow in Britain. Whilst this is obviously dictated by general climatic trends (which vary over thousands of years, hence the ice ages of eons past) the ambient altitude of the "tree line" should certainly be a lot higher than that which is actually found today; forests of sessile oak and native pine should clothe all but the steepest and most inhospitable tops and crags. The overwhelming reason why many of the peaks and heights are not forested today is sheep farming.

"Stone Age Man" began the clearance of the natural forests of England's uplands, chipping away at the wildwood with ineffectual tools and grazing goats and sheep in such small clearings, these ruminants preventing the regeneration of trees in these areas by, simply, eating the young trees as they sprouted.

The Angles and Scandinavian settlers developed such husbandry but it was the monasteries which proved the downfall of the greater part of the forests. These religious foundations made great fortunes from wool, producing much of the wealth that allowed Britannia to rule the waves over several centuries. The million upon million of sheep, aided and abetted by woods being coppiced and felled for charcoal, ensured that the forest shrank and eventually all-but disappeared from much of the Lake District (and the rest of Britain).

The sheep remain a dominant presence today, defeated only by the virtually inedible bracken but still ensuring a tree-free uplands. Those other noticeable features of the uplands, the stone walls, are products of various ages. Some date back to medieval times and some to the times of the Enclosures of the Sixteenth and Eighteenth centuries when lands were "taken in" from common lands, ostensibly to improve agricultural practices but largely to enhance the power and wealth of relatively few individuals at the expense of the rights of many. Still more were built by prisoners of war during the Napoleonic Wars; it was during this period that the greatest proportion of land ever under cultivation in England was farmed, many of the high pastures lined by ruined and fallen walls today were corn or potato fields in 1810.

The thirst for water is the last major player in man's effects on the landscape. Most of the lakes in the Lake District are put to use to supply water for one use or another. Thus Wastwater supplies water to the Sellafield complex on the coast whilst water from Windermere finds it's way to Manchester.

Two of the lakes are artificial. Haweswater was created in the 1930's by Manchester Corporation who dammed Mardale in order to gather and store water for the metropolis; before, Mardale was an isolated, peaceful community nestling in a patchwork of fields beside a much smaller lake. In a similar vein, Thirlmere was developed as a water supply by Manchester in the 1890's. Before then two small lakes, Leathe's Water and Wythburn Water, glistened in the narrow valley to the west of Helvellyn. A dam raised the water level, drowned the village of Armboth and created the one lake we see today.

Together with the artificial screes, levels and holes created by various mining and quarrying operations, the cumulative effect of man on the landscape of the Lake District has been profound in an esoteric sort of way; those with Wordsworth's "eye to perceive" can yet scratch through this manicure to appreciate the body on which it is laid and find vestiges of the untrammelled wilderness.

The Drinking Luminaries of Literary Lakeland

More has been written about the various poets, writers, novelists, commentators – call them what you will – who lived in or were frequent (or not so frequent) visitors to old Westmorland, Cumberland and Lancashire-over-the-Sands than ever was written by all of them put together. Maybe the blame for the deforestation of the fells and valleys should be placed fairly and squarely with these essayists, biographers, scholars and critics rather than sheep, charcoal burners or public and private forestry concerns!

That they made a great contribution to the language, or at least the culture, of Britain is undoubted. Nor can it be doubted that their influence both in attracting visitors (tourists) to this part of North Western England and in encouraging the conservation of the region has been substantial; it's a fair bet that you, reader, read some Arthur Ransome, Beatrix Potter, William Wordsworth or Hugh Walpole long before you ventured to the Lakes and thus had a certain picture or expectation in mind.

Perhaps your expectations and enjoyment of the region will be heightened still further by the knowledge that, in drinking a pint or two in a local pub, you're following in some famous footsteps (or should that be quaffing in some famous tankards...?). After all, these well-to-do folk were only human!

Take the most renowned of all, William Wordsworth, for example. Virtually every building old enough to claim a connection with him (and he only died in 1850) does so, and pubs are no exception. Thus he drank in The George in Keswick (together with Shelley and Coleridge), The Horse and Farrier in Threlkeld and in The Swan in Grasmere. Indeed, he went one better than most and actually lived in a pub; visitors to Dove Cottage are in fact in the old Dove and Olive Branch alehouse. Coleridge and de Quincy are noted as being past customers of The Unicorn in Ambleside whilst Charles Dickens is rumoured to have been seen in the New Hall Inn (Hole in't Wall) in Bowness. Pub grub, too, was enjoyed by literary "names," Nathaniel Hawthorne dined at the Lowwood Hotel on the eastern shore of Windermere whilst Sir Walter Scott regularly took breakfast at The Swan in Grasmere (apparently he didn't appreciate the fare offered by the Wordsworth's). Celia Fiennes, that doyenne of female travellers, was particularly taken by a fish dish – *"At the Kings Arms (Kendal) one Mrs Rowlandson she does pot up the char fish the best of any in the country."*

Arthur Ransome has the distinction of having a beer named after one of his creations; the Masons Arms at Strawberry Bank brews it's own "Amazon" ale, named in favour of Ransome's "Swallows and Amazons" – perhaps the pub should market an "I've Swallowed an Amazon" T-shirt. Ransome spent his final years nearby. Another character in local literary endeavours to have a beer named after him was the incorrigible John Peel, he of the coat so grey. His immortality was ensured by the virtually unknown composer John Woodcock Graves who wrote the famous song in 1832, first performed in The Rising Sun Inn in Caldbeck. The brewers Matthew Brown for many years made a strong bitter which they called John Peel, a beer only phased out in the past year or so.

But it was Mrs William Heelis (a.k.a. Beatrix Potter) who perhaps did more for any one pub than any other personality did for their "local." By drawing a picture of the Tower Bank Arms in Near Sawrey and including this in "The Tale of Jemimah Puddleduck" she ensured literary immortality for this modest village hostel (and as she lived just behind it there's a fair chance that a nip or two of ginger wine might have been supped...).

Keats and Southey, Walpole and Gilpin, Ruskin and Arnold; all took inspiration from the Lake District of their day and from it's inns. Walpole and Wordsworth contrived to mention specific pubs in their work, a practice echoed today by contemporary writers such as Melvyn Bragg, resident of "Back 'o Skiddaw" land and literary benefactor to many a pub in that area, and in Norman Nicholson's prose, poetry and evocation of the very bones and living history of the landscape of the Lakes.

Residents, Tourists and Visitors – Past and Present

Those renowned travellers, the Romans, made a lasting impression on the Lake District, and it certainly was not one beneficial to the earliest inhabitants. These unknown Bronze Age people lived by the land and for the land; their mysterious stone circles, standing stones and cairns were, it is thought, constructed largely to show their veneration for the land, the seasons and Mother Nature. They were the earliest "Greens." Not so the Romans. They had but two purposes, to conquer the local Brigantes peoples and to extract as much mineral wealth as possible from the region. To this end they mined lead, silver, gold, coal, copper and tin from the fells, exporting much of this through ports such as Ravenglass or, via their network of roads, overland to the east coast and south to their more "civilised" domains. The local tribes were decimated. Like the early tourists they were, the Romans came, saw, took and left.

The legacy the Romans left was one of roads, forts, that renowned Wall, rumour of minerals and lands available for colonization. This latter option was taken up during the Dark Ages by Angles and Saxons who left their mark in place names still used today. Villages and towns which include in their names elements such as ton, ing, ham and wick (eg Wigton, Askham, Workington or Urswick) can trace their foundations back to these Germanic peoples. Most of these settlements are on the low lying coastal areas and the flatter lands to the north of the mountains.

And therein lies the reason for this, the Saxons believed that evil spirits dwelled on mountains and in stones. Thus they wouldn't countenance living in stone buildings (this may also be ascribed to the fact that they came from heavily wooded areas of Europe where wood was the be-all and end-all of life) and steered well clear of valleys and hill pastures overshadowed by the dread-mountains.

The settlement of the mountains and valleys was left to the next wave of visitors, those Danes, Vikings and Norse beloved of the rape and pillage school of stage and screen. It appears that nothing could be further from the truth when looking at the Cumbrian Scandinavians. They came not in search of conquest and concubines but of farmland and new homes. It was they who introduced the Herdwick sheep to Britain, upon the backs of which great wealth was later to be based. Again it is through place names that the Norse legacy is most easily seen; thwaites and wicks, waths and grises, scales and thorpes, forces and becks all abound in and around the Lake District and all have a derivation from Scandinavian words for features of the landscape or of nature. Thus Grisedale is a valley of the pigs/swine, Seathwaite is a clearing used as a summer pasture, Sawrey means "wet place" and Scales a temporary shelter.

Their hopes of a peaceful new homeland were dashed for centuries on end by the continual wars between the Scots and the Normans. William the Conqueror took over where the Romans had left off, hoping to push the Scots into the sea; his ancestors and successors continued this quest (Edward the First, for example, died in 1307 whilst on such a quest at Burgh-by-Sands, west of Carlisle), resulting in centuries of devastation and distress for the local populace. The pele towers that are so familiar in the Lake District date from this period, built as places of refuge from lightning raids carried out by malevolent Scots.

During this period the great religious houses all but governed the area, keeping a fragile peace where possible and establishing a solid economic foundation based on the Herdwick sheep. Thus the Abbeys at Shap and Carlisle, Cartmel and Furness, St. Bees and Calder held much of the land and controlled much of the trade, surviving until the dissolution of the monasteries in the Sixteenth Century, the mantle of developing and exploiting the region then passing to the miners, the charcoal burners and the yeoman sheep farmers whose activities will turn up time and time again in the walks featured in this book.

That strange, irrational fear of the mountains instilled by the Angles and Saxons remained engrained in the minds of the vast majority of the population of England until the Eighteenth Century. Only through the ministrations of the poets and writers who adopted the region was the hatred of the dark, loathsome fells and mountains replaced by a growing appreciation of these awesome peaks and lakes. Earlier writers on travel, such as Leland (1500s), Celia Fiennes (1600s) and Daniel Defoe (1700s) all visited this northwest corner of England. Celia Fiennes was overawed but impressed by the scenery – "*As I walked down at this place I was walled on both sides by those inaccessible high rocky barren hills which hangs over ones head in some places and appear very terrible; from these great fells there are several springs out of the rock that trickle down their sides , and as they meet with stones and rocks in the way when something obstructs their passage and so they come with more violence that gives a pleasing sound and murmuring voice."* She was less impressed with the villages in the area, however – "..*villages of sadde little huttes made up of dry walls only stones piled together, there seemed to be no tunnells for their chimnies; I took them at first sight for barns to fodder cattle in."*

Many of the writers who espoused the beauty of the region were also those most vociferously opposed to the development of easier access to their fortress of natural wonders, none more so than Wordsworth or Ruskin who both vehemently opposed the construction of railways aimed at opening up the area. But come the railways did, and with them the droves and droves of tourists and visitors so feared by the poets. The town of Windermere is almost entirely a product of these early days of mass tourism; Ambleside and Keswick gained a much needed new breath of life and these inland resorts became favourite destinations for thousands of excursion trains from the towns and cities of the industrial north – particularly Manchester and the cotton towns of Lancashire to which the Lakes ran a close second to the Blackpool's, Southport's and Morecambe's of this world as a favourite destination.

And if the railways were a harbinger, then the private car was the doom. No detailed account of the rise of the car or its effects needs be chronicled here, and these effects are by no means all detrimental. Whatever your own views on this, the vast majority of the region's visitors get to and travel round the area by car. And that's about 15 million visitors in 1991.

These visitors come to the area for the natural scenery, the watersports, for its reputation (as a candidate for World Heritage Site listing, already bestowed on The Grand Canyon and Ayers Rock, for example) and for the very fact that it is a National Park. This latter point is something of an enigma. An infamous survey undertaken on Dartmoor in the 1970s, based on sedentary visitors (i.e. day-trippers, not walkers) interviewed in car parks at the major countryside sites found that the majority were there simply because it was a National Park. They had little intention of doing anything other than picnicking or sitting in the car and, most revealing of all, many of them parked facing the road or into the car park, not even getting the benefit of a view of the wilderness. One wonders if much the same could be said of today's car borne visitors to the Lakes; next time you pass a car park en-route to one of the pubs in this book sneak a look......things don't change much, do they?!

Bits And Pieces

The Walks And Maps

Each walk in this book contains comprehensive information which should enable you to complete that particular walk without problems. Virtually all the walks follow public rights of way (roads, bridleways, tow-paths, footpaths, etc.) to which you have unrestricted access. Parts of some walks traverse properties owned and managed by The National Trust and The Forestry Commission; there is a de facto (i.e. generally assumed and accepted by all parties) right of access to such areas. There is, tragically and obscenely, a real danger that as Forestry Commission woodland is "privatised" that right of access is extinguished as a consequence. There's obviously no way of divining which woodland will be sold off next so, in years to come, *cave eas pedes...* walker beware. On the rare occasion where the route of a walk is unclear or uses an unofficial path created by frequent use then this is made clear and an alternative outlined where possible.

The titles of each chapter detail the relevant Ordnance Survey (O.S.) "Pathfinder" sheet or Outdoor Leisure sheet (both at $2^1/_2$" to 1 mile scale) for the area in question. Whilst the sketch maps in the book offer a rough idea of the local area, using the relevant O.S. map obviously offers a comprehensive picture of the area and allows you the option to plan alternative routes, short cuts or diversions at your leisure.

The National Park

The Lake District is the largest of the eleven National Parks in England and Wales (Scotland and Ulster have their own separate systems) and the second such area to be set up; it's 880 square miles were designated in 1951, just weeks after the first National Park (The Peak District) was confirmed.

The very title "National Park" is a misnomer as virtually none of the land belongs to the nation. The name was directly imported from the U.S.A. where the world's first National Park, Yellowstone (Wyoming), was designated in 1872, followed by Yosemite (California) in 1890. These vast areas were (and are) truly "National" parks, the lands vested in the State (with apologies to any Amerindians) and set aside to protect the great natural wonders therein. Tourists and visitors were but a harmless novelty, about two thousand saw Yellowstone in 1872, (but about five million did in 1990).

The concept of the setting aside of areas of great natural beauty (and the consequent visitor pressures) is about the only thing the Lake District has in common with a true "National" Park. Only about 4% of the Lake District is publicly owned (courtesy of the Lake District Special Planning Board). The National Trust (a private charity) owns about 28%, North West Water about 7%, and the Forestry Commission about 6%. The rest is in private hands, much of it owned by hill farmers, by financial institutions or in the hands of the landed gentry.

The Lake District Special Planning Board "manages" the National Park. It's a statutory Authority, based in Kendal (but wanting to move to the shores of Windermere) and responsible for planning controls, park rangers and some of the information services available throughout the Park, including the Visitor and Information Centre at Brockhole, north of Windermere. It also has some powers in other areas, such as recreational transport provision and the control of navigation on the lakes. It is also responsible for negotiating access agreements to areas of high moorland and the mountain peaks, and can, on occasions, purchase tracts of land to give the public greater access to countryside areas (the 4% mentioned above, such areas as Torver Common above Coniston or the land between Rydal Water and Grasmere for example). This access, together with the de facto right of access to most National Trust and Forestry Commission land, means that, proportionately, only Dartmoor has more land open to the public for the purpose of walking.

Safety

I've yet to see someone on stilts walking in the Langdale Pikes area, but virtually any other kind of footwear is there to be seen on the mountains, from sandals on Saddleback to high-heels on Harter Fell. More often than not such "walkers" get away with it, but they can be the bane of any rescue organisation's life.

In truth, virtually all the walks in this book could be easily completed using town shoes or, certainly, trainers. But the message is, don't. You wouldn't go canoeing without a paddle or windsurfing without a sail, so don't go hill or fell walking without a decent pair of waterproof, well soled boots. None of the walks climb above 2000 feet but most of them encounter "real" mountain walking – rough tracks, boggy moorland, uneven, heather covered moorland, loose scree and all the other joys of a day in the hills. To tackle such in anything less than footwear designed for the job is plain stupid.

The other thing to ensure you set out with is a decent waterproof. In the Lakes, legion are the days when a glorious bright morning suddenly deteriorates into a misty, wet afternoon. If you're properly equipped then its all part of the fun, but being caught on lowly Loughrigg in nothing but a T-shirt and shorts is not to be recommended. Never forget that, although you're at a relatively low level, you're in mountain country on the majority of walks in this book; treat the terrain with the respect it deserves and you shouldn't have any problems, at least of your own making.

Mountain Rescue

The Mountain Rescue Teams are called out tens, often hundreds of times a year to go to the aid not only of climbers who have fallen but also to walkers and ramblers who have come to grief (and, increasingly, mountain bike riders who have come a cropper). Team members are all volunteers and provide and maintain much of their own equipment, clothing to Landrovers and walkie-talkies. Most of the pubs visited on the walks in this book – and most other pubs in Cumbria – have charity collection boxes on their bars to collect funds for these rescue teams. Please don't ignore them...you never know when **you** may need to call on the services of these volunteers. To contact the Mountain Rescue Team dial 999 and ask for Mountain Rescue (and yes, I know this may prove difficult in the midst of the fells and mountains...).

Public Transport

Being a rural County, the grip on life that the public transport network has in Cumbria is somewhat tenuous, many of the services run only thanks to subsidies from the County Council and these are as fickle as the size of the overall pot into which the public transport section of the Council (or the Special Planning Board) can dip. There is, nonetheless, a reasonable daily service between the main towns operated largely by Cumberland Motor Services (CMS) in the north and Ribble Motors in the south. Mountain Goat run services to many smaller villages and through country areas that would otherwise not see a bus from one month to the next.

In general, there are more services in the summer months (say May to September) than during the rest of the year, buses are more frequent on Mondays to Fridays than at weekends and many routes do not have a Sunday service. At weekends, particularly during the summer, there may be dedicated leisure services, usually run using minibuses, which are of particular value to ramblers.

It would be a spurious addition to the information given in the titles to each walk to detail bus services to the pub in question as such is prone to change at relatively short notice. The answer is to use the County Bus Information Line, telephone **Carlisle (0228) 812812**, where up to the minute timetable information is available for the whole County. You can also, in season, pick up timetable information from any Tourist Information Centre, often in the form of a newspaper detailing services and suggestions for round trips and linear walks.

Rail services are of little use to reach any of the pubs or walks featured in this book. There are only two lines, the Cumbrian Coast Line (around the coast as the name suggests) and the Windermere branch between Oxenholme (near Kendal) and Windermere; on only a handful of occasions do any of the walks come within a couple of miles of a station.

The Walks

Early Spring – a perfect time for walking

Cumberland

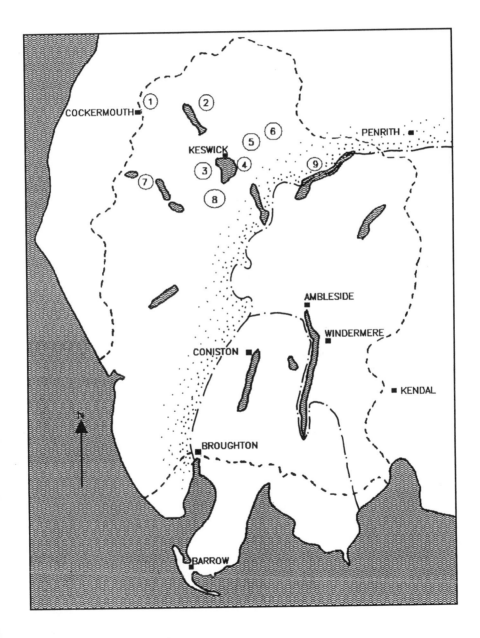

1. Cockermouth

Route: Cockermouth – Watch Hill – Isel – Redmain

Distance: 8 miles

Map: O.S Pathfinder Sheet NY 03/13 Cockermouth and Maryport

Start: The Swan Inn, Kirkgate, Cockermouth. Grid reference: NY 123307

Access: Kirkgate leads directly off the Market Place which is at the eastern end of Main Street, just over the river bridge. Look for All Saints Church and you won't go wrong. The narrow entrance to Kirkgate is just past the Chinese take-away, The Swan Inn is 200 yards up the hill and on the right.

The Swan Inn (0900 822425)

A small, back-street local well worth seeking out in one of the older parts of Cockermouth, the Swan dates from the early 1600s and is one of Jennings's oldest pubs. The Bitter and Cumberland Bitter are dispensed from a small corner bar at one end of the long, low main room, simply furnished with wall seats and decorated with a few old photographs, maps and posters. The bar sports a hop vine trailed above optics and shelves heaving with a vast selection of malt whiskies. There's a small back room used as a family room and bar snacks are available.

Cockermouth

Several of the sons of Cockermouth got a long way in their chosen professions. Wordsworth was born here in 1770, his childhood home is now a museum towards the western end of Main Street. John Dalton, one of the giants of the chemistry and atomic theory world and the discoverer of colour blindness, came from the village of Eaglesfield, just outside Cockermouth. One son got further than most, however. Pitcairn Island to be precise, the lonely Pacific Island where Fletcher Christian and his band of renegades isolated themselves after that mutiny on the Bounty.

They all left behind a thriving market town whose wealth came largely from the woollen industry, for which it was one of the foremost centres in the country. This wealth generated some fine architecture during the Georgian era, much of which survives along the wide, tree lined Main Street and in the maze of passages and side streets that are an integral part of the town's character – Kirkgate and Cocker Lane for example.

The town's history goes back a lot further than to the 1700's, however. There was a Roman fort just northwest of the town and the Normans built a solid sandstone castle at the confluence of the rivers Cocker and Derwent, one of the few castles still being lived in today – it's home to Lord Egremont and occasionally opened to the public. Adjoining the castle is Jennings's brewery, open rather more frequently than the castle with tours available most mornings and afternoons.

The Walk

Return to the Market Place and turn right up the short, steep bank at the bottom of Castlegate. Remain with this road and walk gradually uphill and out of the town, eventually passing by Cockermouth School on your left. A short distance later pass the entrance to Wyndham Holiday Park on your right and continue along the main road until you come to a bridleway sign on the left pointing the way to Isel Bridge – it's about a hundred yards before the road junction so if you reach this you've gone too far!

Go through the green gate into the field and take the right hand field track, starting a long steady climb up to the summit of Watch Hill. Initially you're heading for some isolated brick walls in the middle of a field, before you reach these go through the green field gate on your right and stick with the rough field road, aiming for the small plantation visible some way ahead. As you climb the stile to the left of this woodland so you enter the National Park; a glance behind at this point offers an excellent view over Cockermouth, huddled in its bowl formed at the confluence of the Derwent and Cocker rivers.

Simply remain with the wide track and continue the stroll up to the summit of Watch Hill, at 770 feet a modest height but one blessed with incredible views. The highest point is that just to the right of this end of the large tract of woodland you reach, immediately above the small old

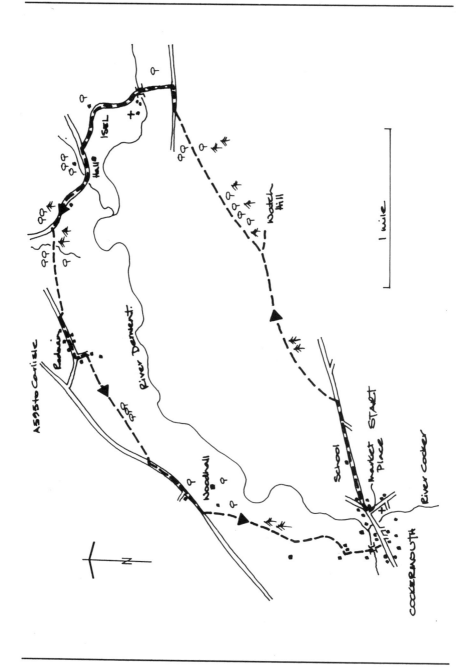

workings. From this summit look north across the undulating northern Cumbrian countryside to the Solway Firth and, beyond this, the mountains of Dumfries and Galloway. To the west the sea glints at Workington whilst to the south is a fulsome panorama of the mountains of the northern Lake District: Skiddaw, Grisedale Pike, Grasmoor, High Stile, Red Pike and many other peaks familiar to most fell walkers. Slightly less familiar, perhaps, are those on the right as you look south, Fellbarrow, Mellbreak and the other outlying tops of the Loweswater Fells. Completing the sweep through the points of the compass, to the east are the lonely, rounded summits of "Back o' Skiddaw", Great Calva, Knott, Binsey and the Uldale and Caldbeck Fells.

To find the path down from Watch Hill walk to the corner of the woods, here badly affected by storm damage, and walk along the line of the fence on your right. In fifty or so yards is a stile beside a gate on your right; climb this and join the rough road which winds into the woodland. This is the same track you've been following for the past mile or so, simply remain with it and ignore any tracks off to the right. A further mile or so's walk in and alongside the mixed birch, oak and fir trees brings you to a minor road. Walk straight ahead along this and, in a couple of hundred yards or so, turn left at the junction signposted for Blindcrake, Sunderland and Isel and walk down to the old bridge across the Derwent.

Once across this bear left with the road and walk around the corner. On the left here is the driveway leading down to the church of St. Michael and All Angels, a short detour not to be missed. This is another of those incredibly old churches that old Cumberland seems to have round almost every corner. This one was built in about 1130 and, despite the seemingly inevitable attentions of the Victorians, largely retains its fine Norman architecture. The tiny windows on the north wall show just how thick the walls are whilst the rough-hewn beams and rafters have probably never been replaced since construction. There are old wall monuments dating from the 1600's and a couple of bricked-up doorways which suggest that those early Cumbrians must have been pygmies. Look, too, for the three fragments of old carved stones found in and around the church in years gone by. One of these, the Triskele Stone, may be a part of an early Christian cross dating back to the Dark Ages, around 1500 years ago.

There seems to be a local practice of walking along the riverside to the splendid old Isel Hall, visible in the middle distance, but as no public right of way seems to exist return to the minor road and bear left, in half a mile or so reaching Isel Hall on your left. It's a private house, essentially an Elizabethan mansion built around a pele tower and with later additions such as the walled garden. An early resident was a Sir William Leigh. When he died in 1354 he was buried in the churchyard at St. Michael's Church......as was his favourite horse. You can't really see much from the road, so continue ahead, ignoring the road to the right. There are a few estate buildings scattered here and there including, back to your right, the old mill.

Cross the stream and wind uphill for the next mile or so, passing by the old village school, dated 1836 and now a private house. Walk along the long straight beyond the school and reach an area of woodland on your left. Keep your eyes peeled for the public footpath sign for Redmain, on the left about two hundred yards up the woodland edge. Go along this, at first very overgrown but then more obvious as it flits from glade to glade in the deciduous woods, keeping the fir plantation off to the left. Cross the braided brook on the two little footbridges and walk on through to the edge of the woods, leaving them via the stile beneath the large oak. Keep an ear out for the "mewing" call of Buzzards which are common hereabouts.

Head straight across the large field you're now in, using the pairs of treestumps as a rough directional guide. Climb the next stile beside a tall pole and continue on the same line across this next huge field. At the far side look for the offset corner of the hedge about half way down, marked by a large elder bush. By this is a small wooden stile and beyond this a gap stile. Once through this climb the bank ahead and on your right and then head for the tall ash and oak trees in the far corner. Beneath these is another gap stile, cross through this and scramble up the bank beyond to the minor road, turning left along this to reach the hamlet of Redmain.

This is no more than a strand of very old cottages and farms strung along this quiet back road. At the far end of the hamlet, just before the point where the road bends right past a white cottage with black-painted window lintels and surrounds, a farm drive falls away to the left. This is the drive to Redmain Lodge, walk down it, past the old farm on your left and the barn on your right. Go through the rickety old gate and along the field road beyond, initially sticking to the right of the little limestone crag and passing by the site of an old pond. In a short distance the track splits and a deeply furrowed track climbs the cragside to your left. Walk up this to the top of the crag and then walk along the limestone ridge to the corner of the woods ahead. Climb the stile here and walk on, keeping these woods on your left. Cross a further stile and continue to the point where the woods fall away to the left just beyond a small, deep gully. Here slightly favour your right hand and walk across the pasture to the small crag capped with a few ash and oak. Just to the left of this is a further stile to cross, once over which look to your right to locate the gate through the wall, about one hundred yards away. Go through this and turn left, walking out of this lay-by and onto the verge of the busy A595 road.

Cross the road to the wider verge and remain with this very busy road for nearly half a mile. Once you've passed the house and bungalow on your right (on a cut-off from the main road) recross the road and look on the left for a public footpath sign, about fifty yards beyond the drive to Woodhall Farm. Cross the stone step stile here and walk along the top ridge of the pasture, shortly crossing a further stile at the corner of a plantation then continuing down through the parkland, the plantation on your left. Cross straight over the estate road (there's a lodge house some yards off to your left) and bear half right. Ahead you'll see a bridge across a beck, walk down to but don't cross it. Instead walk a few yards to the right to the corner of a fence and turn left here, walking up over the parkland with this fence on your left.

Climb the stone step stile at the far end of the fence and walk on, woodland on your left. There are several more stone step stiles to cross and you'll end up heading virtually directly for the tower at Jennings's brewery in central Cockermouth. When you reach the double metal gate through a hedge head towards the tall mill chimney below you and soon the final part of the route will become obvious, it's the old hedged, green lane gained by passing through the gap stile at your end of it. Follow this old lane until you reach the left turn just beyond the derelict mill on your left. Turn along here and walk back into Cockermouth, crossing the Derwent on the footbridge just a few yards from the Main Street.

2. Bassenthwaite

Route: Bassenthwaite – Ullock Pike Foot – Lakeside – Scarness

Distance: 7 miles

Map: O.S.Pathfinder sheet NY23/33 Caldbeck and Outdoor Leisure Sheet 4, The English Lakes NW.

Start: Bassenthwaite Village. Grid reference: NY 232324

Access: Bassenthwaite is about two miles to the east of the tip of the lake of the same name and is signposted from the A591 Keswick to Bothel road. Park at the pub or around the village green.

The Sun Inn (07687 76439)

Bassenthwaite is the "wrong" side of Keswick, away from the mainstream tourist routes and refreshingly uncluttered, unlike villages of a similar size in the heart of the Lake District. The village pub, The Sun Inn, lies at the heart of this ancient community, behind one of the village centre farms and opposite the old mill. It was once a farm itself, evidenced by a quick glance along the side of the main building. Within, the old waist level panelling is all but hidden behind wall benches which provide much of the seating in the main bar, an area of nooks and crannies curving round three sides of the large central bar. Contorted, darkened beams give clue to the age of the building as do the small, leaded windows at the front which overlook a small patio housing a couple of tables. If the weather's fit this is a relaxing place to sit, the sound of the nearby Dash Beck adding its voice to the occasional farmyard cacophony and with the heights of the Uldale Fells climbing steeply from the village edge painting a stunning visual backdrop.

Off the main bar room is a long thin room housing the menu blackboard, the choice on which varies daily – the pub has a good name for the quality and quantity of bar meals; food is served from 12 noon-1.30pm and 6.30pm-8.30pm. The pub's decor includes a large number of old bottles, local watercolours and a 1958 bar prices list enough to make your eyes water. Several fireplaces guarantee a warm haven from the northern hills and fells during the winter months, Jennings' Bitter being the beer available to quench that thirst.

The Walk

With your back to the pub's facade walk along the lane and curve right with it, passing one of the farms and a row of old cottages to reach the village green. Immediately on reaching this green turn left and walk towards the appropriately named Green Cottage. On your left you may notice a bridleway sign for Peter House Farm. Turn left again in front of Green Cottage and walk up along the lane past the cottages and bungalows, bearing right at the top and walking along to the field gate at the end. Climb the stile beside this and look to the far side of the pasture, aiming to walk to the tallest tree beneath which is a further stile. You're walking directly towards the highest point of the Skiddaw range at 3054 feet, the rather sharp peak just to the right is Ullock Pike.

Climb the stile and head for the telegraph pole at the far end of the field, in line with the farm ahead. At this corner is a narrow gate beneath the pole; go through this and walk down the meadow to the minor road, turning left along this. Remain with it, pass the farm and wind round a couple of bends to reach a wooded area on your right. Here, a public footpath sign points over a stile and into the woods. Follow this path, cross the little wooden footbridge and climb up the zig-zag path on the far side, walking along the edge of the woods for a short while before entering a long thin pasture on your left. Stick to the left side of this pasture and walk up to the minor road at the top. Cross straight over this and walk ahead along the rough drive leading to Hole House Farm.

Walk between the house and the far barn and on for a few yards to reach a bridleway sign pointing up to the right, then follow this directional indicator to the top of the slope. Beside the gate at the top you'll find a permissive path sign (painted on a piece of slate). Bear left with this and follow the line of fence, keeping it to your right. At the far end climb the ladder stile (it's very boggy on the far side) and turn right up the wide green track. Cross the stile and continue straight ahead, the farm and barn on your right. Shortly, climb the ladder stile and follow the sunken track across the field to a stand of sycamores. Continue

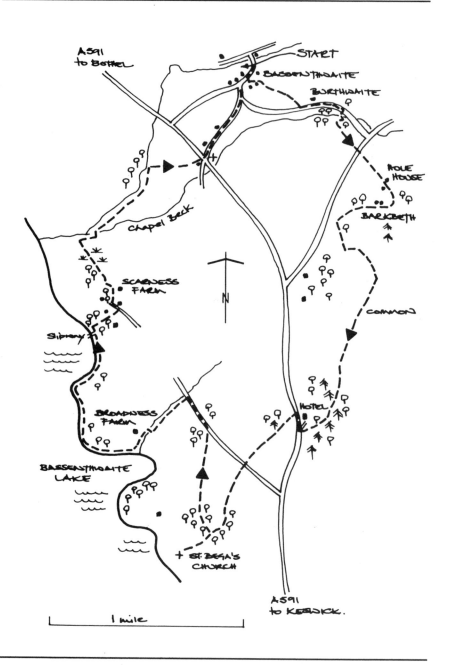

round the snout of the hill on your left and look for the gate in the wall. Once through this walk gradually downhill to the line of threadbare hedge which threads its way up the fellside to your left. Follow this hedge uphill and out beyond up the path to the small waymarker post, turning left here to find a ladder stile across the wall. Once over this turn right and walk up over the craggy pasture to the wall at the narrow top end of the field.

The wall here marks the lower edge of Bassenthwaite Common. Climb the ladder stile and bear right, roughly following the line of the wall on your right. So long as you keep the line of this wall in mind its worth climbing a little higher up the hillside (the lower slopes of Ullock Pike) to better appreciate the views over Bassenthwaite Lake which is ahead (west) of you, a patchwork of tiny fields and marshy pastures filling the low lying area between the lake and the fell foot. The wall eventually meets the top corner of a woodland plantation and it is for this corner that you should aim if you're some distance up the fellside on one of the many sheep tracks.

Bassenthwaite Panorama, from the foot of Ullock Pike

Remain outside the plantation and follow the path down, the trees to your right. Go through the gate at the end, wind down to and cross the forest road and follow the steep, narrow path down through a further area of woods, passing through the gate and remaining with this increasingly steep path to emerge onto the A591 beside the entrance to the drive to the Ravenstone Hotel. Turn right along the road and follow it for a hundred yards or so. Opposite the northern driveway entrance to the Hotel look for the footpath sign on your left, pointing down a narrow path behind the drive to Ravenstone Lodge. Go down this and walk along the line of huge pines to the kissing gate at the far end, just beyond the last pine and a chestnut tree (i.e. not the first gate on your right). Once through the gate walk across the pasture, cross the stile and brook and wind through the area of oak and thorn to a gate at the far side. Pass through a line of kissing gates to reach a minor road, go straight over this and along the field road opposite signposted for St. Bega's Church.

The church is approached along a long avenue of massive oak trees, themselves ancient but no match for the age of the church which dates back to Saxon times, although remains from that era are scant. Some fine Norman stonework – the chancel arch for example – survived the Victorian restorers who practiced their art in 1874, late enough for Tennyson to have enjoyed the original, unscathed creation. He stayed with the Spedding family at nearby Mirehouse (which you can see from the circular churchyard) and is said to have gained inspiration for parts of his retelling of the Arthurian Legend – "Morte d'Arthur" – from St. Bega's, presumed to be the "Chapel in the Fields" in the epic poem. Bassenthwaite Lake itself is his candidate for the stretch of water from which a hand emerged to catch the sword Excalibur, flung by Arthur as his final act. One of the Knights of Arthur's Round Table, Sir Gawaine, also passed this way on his quest for the Green Knight, which quest ended at the Solway Firth, not a million miles away. St. Bega was an Irish nun who fled her homeland, first founding St. Bees monastery (strange how a nun should found a monastery...) on the coast before travelling inland to establish a church at this isolated lakeside spot.

Retrace your steps from the church and walk back up the avenue of oaks to the first bend to the right. Here, look left across the pasture to the area of woodland to find a stile giving access to these woods. Walk through the woods, across the pasture at the far side and into a further plantation. Wind with the overgrown path through these trees to emerge in a further large pasture. Look out here for buzzards hunting these woodlands and lakeside marshes and, grazing in the reedbeds between the lake and the pasture, glimpses of the shy red deer which live in the area. Go through the field gate at the far side of this first pasture and straight across the subsequent larger field, heading for the tall ash tree on the far side. Pass through the kissing gate here, cross the farm road and enter the field opposite, then heading for the opposite right hand corner (to the right of the woods) where a stile gives access to a minor road. Turn left along this and follow it for about two hundred yards to a public footpath sign on your left.

Take this path, following the course of a little brook on your right, and head towards the farm some distance away. The brookside is generously blessed with umpteen wildflowers, red Bistort, yellow Trefoil, blue and purple Vetches, the pungent white Meadowsweet, Deadnettles, Forget-me-nots and purple Knapweed to name but a few, the brook itself has various crowfoots and lilies. Cross the footbridge and remain with the overgrown path to, eventually, reach a stile some little distance to the left of the farm. Climb this and turn left, walking down to the lake shore. For the next mile and a half remain with the lake shore, climbing a number of stiles in the process. If the wind is from the west you'll notice an annoying rumble of traffic from the A66 which runs up alongside the opposite, west, shore but, this apart, the lake is peaceful, quiet and overshadowed by the fine fells and crags of Sale Fell, Broom Fell and the curiously-named Barf. Fences disappear into the water as if old pastures had been drowned and occasional dinghy racing disturbs the tranquillity of this much-undervisited sheet of water.

When you reach the landing stage walk across the "slipway" and through the gate at the far side, entering a strip of woodland. A few paces into the trees, and just before the gate at the far side, turn right up the obvious path and walk up this strip of woods between the chalet parks here at Scarness. On reaching the road at the top turn left and follow the road (n.b. not the drive to Bassenthwaite Lodges), in a short while bearing right up the well tended driveway of Scarness Farm (a notice says Private Road but it is a public footpath). Where this bears right towards the farm go straight ahead, pass to the left of the black barn and bear gradually left to enter the field. You need to go to the opposite corner of this field, so head half right, aiming for the right hand corner of the woods ahead. At the bottom corner of the field cross the wide bridge and go through the gate. Walk ahead now across the somewhat boggy area, keeping the fence on your left, and pass through the kissing gate at the end. Beyond this is a footbridge; don't cross this but turn right at your end of it and walk along the narrow beckside path, following Chapel Beck upstream.

Bassenthwaite Lake: peaceful, quiet and overshadowed by fine fells and crags

Cross the next footbridge you reach and turn right, for a short distance there's a stream either side of you but the one on your right, Chapel Beck, soon disappears into the meadows. Remain with the other stream on your left and follow it upstream for a further few hundred yards to the point where an old packhorse bridge crosses it. At this point look to your right to find the sharp corner of a hedge and walk to this, beyond which a line of stiles aligned with the church spire in the middle distance marks the route to follow. Look carefully at the hedge as you reach it – it's formed from diminutive ash trees which have been trained and grafted together over the years to form a very strong boundary.

Walk along the line of stiles towards the church, on entering the last field head for the far left hand corner, just to the left of the white-painted cottage. Cross straight over the crossroads here, down past the tiny chapel on your right and follow this lane back to Bassenthwaite village a further half mile away.

The Sun, Bassenthwaite

3. Barrow Gill

Route: Swinside – Little Braithwaite – High Coledale – Barrow Door

Distance: 5 miles

Map: O.S. Outdoor Leisure Series Sheet 4, The English Lakes NW

Start: Swinside Inn. Grid reference: NY 243217

Access: From Keswick follow the Cockermouth Road to the A66 and then, in about 200 yards, turn off the A66 into Portinscale village, a turn signposted for Portinscale, Grange and Buttermere. Follow the signs for Grange along these narrow roads for about two miles, then bear right at the sign for Stair. The Swinside Inn is on the right about 200 yards past this junction.

Swinside Inn (07687 78253)

Swinside is an afforested crag at the north west end of Derwent Water, planted with an assortment of fir trees interspersed with occasional oak and birch. It has given its name to a farm and a pub, the only buildings at the settlement of Swinside. At the foot of the crag and on a terrace above Newlands Beck, the Swinside Inn's terrace is the perfect place to sup a pint of Jennings' Bitter on a summer's evening. Across the valley Causey Pike, Grisedale Pike, Stile End and other peaks of "Above Derwent" form a grand horizon near enough to touch whilst to the south down Newlands Valley the sharp ridge of High Crags draws the eye to the top of Hindscarth and, beyond this, the promise of the mighty Great Gable.

The pub itself is a long, low old building, comfortably refurbished to cater for the wide variety of users that venture to this side of Derwent Water. It's very much oriented towards families; beyond the terrace and in the car park is an enclosure housing various fauna, including a raucous peacock, whilst a goat and tame sheep seem to have the run of the place.

The Swinside Inn: the perfect place to sup a pint on a summer's evening

Inside, the pub is open plan, furnished with mocquette wall benches and stools and with a restrained number of wall decorations (brasses, prints and suchlike). Part of the slate slabbed floor has been carpeted and there is a separate games room set in a room behind the bar. The pub has a good reputation for food, specialities include baked trout and beef in ale.

In summer the pub is open from 11am-11pm with food available throughout the day and up to 8.30pm. Winter hours are likely to be more restricted than this, with evening opening at 7pm. The actual entrance to the bar is off the terrace, which is around at the back of the pub and can't be seen from the road or outer car park, so persevere in your quest for a pint or two of Jennings!

The Walk

Walk downhill from the pub, past the farm on your left and to the bend in the road about a hundred yards away. Here, take the rough track off to the right and follow this down onto the valley floor, winding along between the hedges. In a while the track emerges into an open field; bear right with it and follow it across this pasture, turning left at the far side and following the line of hedge round to the corner of the field. Go through the gate here and then walk along the track beside Newlands Beck, following this downstream (n.b. do NOT go through the stile beside this gate and thus follow the beck upstream!).

Don't cross the bridge you reach, instead bear right your side of it and remain with the beck for the next mile or so, Skiddaw looming ever larger ahead of you. When you get to the next bridge join the minor road here, walk across the bridge and up along the road through Little Braithwaite. Carry straight on at the junction, soon passing by a bench on your left. Not far past this, as the road starts to descend, look on the left for a public footpath sign high up in the hedge. Climb the steps here, cross the fence and walk ahead keeping the fence on your right.

A view over Newlands Valley

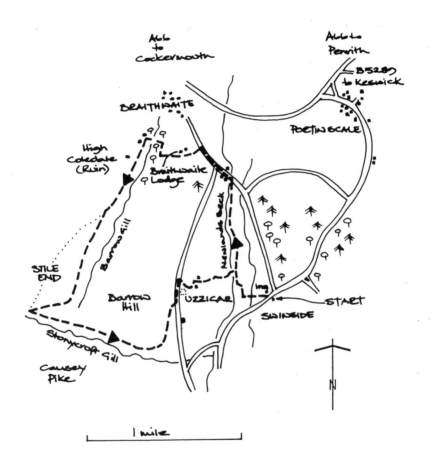

You'll soon reach Braithwaite Lodge, an isolated farm at the foot of the tongue of land that is Barrow hill. There's a crossing of paths at the corner of the yard here, you need to continue westwards in the direction you're already heading, following the only footpath sign at this junction graced by a yellow waymark arrow. Walk across the field to the far side to find a further waymark attached to a gate. Turn right here and walk down alongside the fence to the stile in the bottom corner of the field. Climb this and walk straight across the field towards the woods. You'll reach these woods at a corner. Go down the steep bank here, the woods fenced in to your left, to find a small footbridge beneath the trees. Cross this, Barrow Gill, and scramble up the bank ahead, bearing right at the top to arrive at the pink-painted cottage a few yards away. Turn left along the lane here and commence the steady climb up the valley of Barrow Gill.

Continue on up this lane which, once through the gate, becomes a rough moorland road. At the point where this bends right to reach the now-ruined High Coledale farm go straight ahead up the obvious path and walk on uphill following the course of the Gill. To your right is the deep valley of Coledale Beck, dominated by the peak of Grisedale Pike (2593 feet). You'll soon reach a point at the foot of the spur which is Stile End where the path splits. If you're feeling energetic then take the right fork and scramble up the spur to the top of Stile End. If you prefer a less demanding ramble, however, then favour the left fork and continue up the path which curves around this eastern edge of Stile End. On your left the long fell is Barrow hill whilst ahead Causey Pike looms large just beyond the bwlch (pass).

At the top of the valley the path goes through this pass between Barrow and Stile End, a pass known as Barrow Door. At this point bear half right and follow the path which winds around the end of Stile End opening up fine views ahead up towards Crag Hill, Stonycroft Gill a tiny stream far down to your left. It is for this stream that you are heading, so remain with the path which imperceptibly looses height as you walk up towards the higher peaks. You'll eventually meet the wide track coming down from Crag Hill at a sharp angle, at which point turn back-left and follow this wider track down out of the hills. This junction is the spot to head for if you took the higher route over the summit of Stile End.

There's a splendid view down Stonycroft Gill to the isolated Skelgill Farm at the foot of Cat Bells, to the left of which is a glimpse of Derwent Water; the horizon includes the heights of Matterdale Common, Great Dodd and Stybarrow Dodd. Remain with this track, bearing left with it at the end of the valley and walking gradually down to the minor road. Continue ahead along this for about two hundred yards. Don't be tempted to walk on the scrubby area on your right, this is the site of Barrow copper mine and the overgrown workings are dangerous.

Turn right along the rough driveway to Uzzicar Farm. Go through the first gate at the point where a choice of path is indicated and walk up the tarred drive to the farmyard gate. Here, turn left and walk along the track to Low Uzzicar, passing this by on your left. Stick with this track as it winds through the valley floor meadows and cross the bridge at the end. At this point turn right and rejoin the first part of the walk, retracing your steps along the field road and back up to the Swinside Inn.

Causey Pike from Barrow Gill

4. Walla Crag

Route: Keswick – Springs Farm – Castlerigg Stone Circle – Walla Crag – Lakeside

Distance: About 7 miles

Map: O.S. Outdoor Leisure Series Sheet 4, The English Lakes N.W.

Start: Keswick Town Centre. Grid reference: NY 266234

The Dog and Gun (07687 73463)

Viewed from the outside this old pub on Lake Road is a jumble of levels vieing with its neighbours to receive its share of daylight through its small, flower bedecked windows. Inside, the one large room is a lot less gloomy than its situation would lead you to expect. The main area has a worn, slate flagged floor, sheltered by a low-beamed ceiling, which beams drip with coins of the realm inserted by past visitors; the number of realms represented reflects both the variety of nationalities which visit Keswick and the popularity of the pub.

It's a favourite haunt of climbers and ramblers and the walls are decorated with an abundance of old photographs of the hills and climbs of the Lake District taken by the renowned early local photographers G.P. Abrahams. There are also a few scenes of old Keswick and surrounding villages and a mounted collection of banknotes.

The open plan bar is split into three distinct areas, one carpeted, one slate floored and one with well polished floorboards. The arrangement of the seats results in a large number of alcoves separated by high-backed benches and a forest's worth of small tables. There's also a strange staircase ascending from a point opposite the main door, either partially blocked off by wood panelling or designed to be used, comfortably, by persons of very restricted growth.

The Dog and Gun is a Scottish and Newcastle house offering the standard choice of Theakstons beers which must have been the reason why S&N bought the brewery – Old Peculier, XB and Best Bitter. It's open all day in summer with slightly more restricted hours during the winter (i.e. usually closed for an hour or so during the late afternoon).

Keswick

The capital of the northern Lakes and one of the most popular inland resorts in England, Keswick largely owes its existence to the wool trade. Its market charter dates from the 1200s, after which the town grew rapidly on the backs of the Herdwick sheep raised by the tenant farmers of Fountains Abbey, in distant Yorkshire, who owned all the lands hereabouts. The renowned wool and sheep market will have been held in the Market Place, the centre-piece of which is the Moot Hall, a nineteenth century construction on the site of the original market hall. Off the streets which surround the Market Place are many narrow alleyways leading to back yards. These yards and alleys could be easily blocked off and used as holding pens for the sheep before (and after) they went under the hammer. These back yards and alleyways are part of the charm of Keswick, although most of them are now lined with exclusive shops and restaurants.

Copper mining became important to the local economy in the Sixteenth Century. The first mine was licensed in 1565 in the Newlands Valley, west of the lake. It was worked by German miners, renowned throughout Europe as the creme of the profession. So began a long association between Keswick and extractive industries, lead, gold and silver all being won from the surrounding fells which are to this day littered with the remains of old buildings, shafts, tramways and ropeways. By far the most famous product of the area was graphite, discovered in the Borrowdale Valley and used for an amazing variety of purposes, from a health cure to a lubricant. It's most familiar use, however, was that as the "lead" in lead pencils. The first ones were made in the 1500's and the pencil industry became the town's major employer. The works still thrive and tours are regularly organised. The "lead", however, now comes from abroad.

For well over a century tourism has been the main industry in the town. Most of the rather sombre, slate houses, villas and mansions are

Victorian, many purpose built as hotels and guest houses, although there are occasional older buildings, mostly tucked away in the Yards off the main street. The oldest Inn is The George, an old coaching Inn dating back to Stuart times. Older by far is St Kentigern's Church, set amidst the meadows to the north-west of the town and which traces a history back to its foundation in 553 by St. Kentigern. Amongst the residents of the graveyard is Canon Rawnsley, one of the founders of the National Trust.

The Walk

You should leave the centre of Keswick along Ambleside Road (from the Dog and Gun turn right along Lake Road, turn left up Derwent Street [opposite Fishers] and right at the top along St. John's Street which shortly becomes Ambleside Road). Follow this for several hundred yards until you reach Springs Road on your right; join this and follow it through to its very end at Springs Farm.

Swing left with the track between the farm buildings, go through the gate beside the barn and walk up the rough track through the woodlands, keeping the beck in the deep valley on your left. In a short while, at the point where you can see a footbridge in the trees ahead of you, turn sharp right and follow the path signposted for Castlerigg. The path soon swings left and hugs the edge of the woodland, to your right extensive views open out across Derwent Water to the Derwent Fells and over Borrowdale towards the highest peaks in the Lake District.

Continue uphill with Brockle Beck on your left, shortly passing by a small transmitter station. Ignore any turns to the right and remain with the beck until you reach a footbridge on your left. Cross this and walk up the bank beyond to the surfaced farm road. Turn left along this and, in a matter of yards, go right over the ladder stile and follow the footpath alongside a wall to your left, on the other side of which is a camp-site. Go through the gate at the end and carry on to the next ladder stile, beside which is a signpost for Castlerigg. Climb the stile and turn left, then keeping the line of fence to your left and walking along the old field track virtually (in line of sight) towards the gash in the fellside ahead, Glenderaterra Beck, which separates Lonscale Fell and Skiddaw (left) from Blencathra (Saddleback, right). To your left are

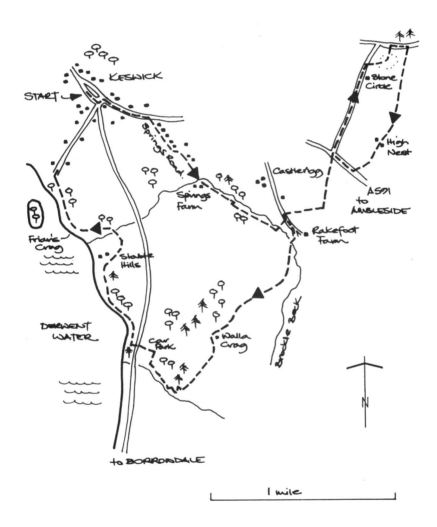

START

KESWICK

Springs Road

Springs Farm

Castlerigg

Stone Circle

High Nest

A591 to AMBLESIDE

Rakefoot Farm

Friar's Crag

Stable Hills

DERWENT WATER

Car Park

Walla Crag

Brockle Beck

to BORROWDALE

1 mile

N

distant views across the northernmost of the region's lakes, Bassenthwaite.

Climb over several stiles, always keeping the fence on your left, and eventually you'll reach the main A591 road. Cross straight over this and walk along the narrow minor road opposite which is signposted for Castlerigg. This is Castle Lane and will bring you, in something over half a mile, to Castlerigg Stone Circle; a footpath sign on your right soon after the small stone barn marks the stile into the pasture which houses this relic. Apart from Stonehenge, Avebury and Silbury Hill in Wiltshire and the Callanish Standing Stones in the Hebrides, Castlerigg Stone Circle is undoubtedly the most spectacular megalithic site in the U.K. It's site is certainly the most dramatic, on a low, windswept hilltop, overshadowed by the Skiddaw Massif to the north, Matterdale Common to the south-east and with distant views further eastwards up and beyond the shallow Glenderamackin Valley to Milburn Forest and Cross Fell, highest point in the Pennines.

Castlerigg Stone Circle has stood since megalithic times in the shadows of Blencathra

There are 38 stones in the main circle. Ten smaller stones form a rectangle within the circle at a point aligned with nearby Threlkeld Knott, a hilltop which, observers suggest, marks the equinoctial sunrise; as with virtually all stone circles and similar monuments, close connection with the seasons is suspected as the *raison d'être* of Castlerigg.

From the Circle walk across the field directly towards distant Blencathra, almost immediately reaching a minor road (and, quite possibly, a few cars parked on a rough roadside car-park). Turn right and walk along this road for a hundred yards or so. At the bend, opposite a stand of Caledonian Pines, go through the gate on the right, a public footpath sign indicating a path to High Nest. Initially, keep the wall on your right and then walk virtually straight towards the highest hill ahead, Bleaberry Fell. A line of ladder stiles will take you past a stand of fir trees to a gate leading into the farmyard of High Nest. Walk through the farmyard and along the driveway beyond, soon reaching the A591. Cross this busy road and turn right, walking up the pavement to the signpost for Walla Crag on your left. Go through the gate here and retrace your earlier steps back to the surfaced farm road just past the camp-site.

Turn left along this road and walk to the fork, here bearing right towards Walla Crag. At the end of the lane cross the footbridge and bear left, starting the climb up the fellside to the summit of the crag. Keep the wall to your right, pass through a gate after a while, marking the boundary of the National Trust's Castlerigg property, and continue up the well used path. Near the top go through the gate on your right and scramble up the remaining few yards to the summit of Walla Crag, 1234 feet above sea level.

This is a famous viewpoint, visited by thousands of walkers each year eager to experience the glorious panorama of the Derwent Fells and Derwent Water, Great Gable and Scafell. Perhaps the most unsung vista from here (and for which you should choose the clearest of days) is the distant one up the length of Bassenthwaite and across the Solway Firth to the mountains of Galloway in southern Scotland; Criffel, at 1868 feet is the highest of these, the smudge beyond this being the Forest of Ae above Dumfries, nearly fifty miles away.

*Derwent Water and Bassenthwaite: On a clear day you can see as far as
Galloway from the summit of Walla Crag*

Walk south from the summit and cross the stile over the wall. Turn right and walk gradually downhill, always keeping the wall close to your right hand side and ignoring the main path which diverges off left to Falcon Crags, Bleaberry Fell and Ashness Bridge. After a couple of hundred yards the path becomes very steep, necessitating a short scramble down alongside the wall. At the corner turn right with the wall and then follow the steep, zig-zagging path down, a path largely secured by cut, felled pines, rough steps and slabs which can be extremely slippery in wet weather.

Pass through the gate to enter the woodland, remaining with the path which follows the rushing, waterfall-strewn Cat Gill in a deep defile down to the left. At the break of slope bear half right through the woods, ignoring the footbridge down to your left, and walk down to the car park, on your left a few hundred yards away. Go through the gate and walk directly ahead across the car park, then bear right with the path and walk through the trees to the gap stile beside the road. Cross straight over and walk onto the pebbly shore of Derwentwater here at Calfclose Bay.

Turn right and follow the lakeshore path as it darts into small bays and across wooded promontories. At one point the path leaves the shore to pass behind a few cottages, Stable Hills. Simply follow the driveway away from the cottages for about a hundred yards and then take the path on your left which leaves the drive via a gate beneath a stand of Birch and Ash trees. Remain with the path across Friars Crag to return to the centre of Keswick about half a mile further on.

5. The Greta Valley and Latrigg

Route: Threlkeld – Blencathra Centre – Latrigg – Keswick

Distance: 5 miles

Start: Threlkeld village centre. Grid reference: NY 325255

Map: O.S. Outdoor Leisure Series Sheet 4, The English Lakes NW

Access: I've based this walk on access by bus. There are four or five buses a day (service 104 Keswick – Penrith – Carlisle) from Keswick Bus Station to Threlkeld (but few on Sundays); telephone Cumbria Motor Services on Penrith (0768) 63616 for details. In 1991 the most convenient bus to use was the 1345 from Keswick, arriving in Threlkeld at 1357. Keswick Bus Station is on The Headlands, to the north west of the town centre. Threlkeld village itself is off the A66 about four miles east of Keswick.

The Pubs

Arriving in Threlkeld by bus offers the perfect opportunity to try out a few beers without the worry of having to drive afterwards...and as Threlkeld has two superb little pubs to offer the discerning rambler it would be churlish, to say the least, not to feature them both. The bus stops midway between the two pubs which are all of a hundred yards apart on Threlkeld's one main street.

The **Horse and Farrier** (07687 79688) was built in 1688, the year of the "Glorious Revolution." A glorious revolution it must indeed have been for local drinkers when the Lord of the Manor, one Christopher Irton, had the pub built – his (and his wife's) initials are marked on the lintel above the front door – to cater for the workers on his estate. Many features of that day remain virtually unchanged. The long, low white pub has one large downstairs room, heavily beamed and decorated with hunting prints, photographs and memorabilia courtesy of the Blencathra Hunt which is based at kennels just a few hundred yards away and which regularly takes a stirrup cup at the villages' two pubs. In a display cabinet in one corner of the room is a massive solid silver cup presented to a past Master of the Hunt for long service (or whatever the correct hunting term may be...). The pub also has connections with fell running, a former licensee was a champion at the sport. On offer are Jennings Bitter and Cumberland Bitter (also brewed by Jennings). There's a separate pool room to the right of the bar, wall decorations here include a case of African butterflies presented to a former licensee.

The **Salutation** (07687 79614) is the other village local. This splendid establishment is a Scottish and Newcastle tied house, offering Youngers Scotch Bitter, Theakstons Best, XB and Old Peculier. The bar all but fills the main room, leaving just enough room for a passageway leading to a small back room, a large quarry tiled standing area and a small, carpeted seating area huddled around the fireplace. A roaring fire and a pint or two of Old Peculier on a winters afternoon and you'd never want to leave. It's yet another "long, low beamed" pub, in common with the rest of the local country pubs around here displaying hunting prints, photo's and cartoons – these latter are done by an 84 year old cartoonist from Keswick and can be found wherever there is a connection with the Blencathra Hunt.

Not content with displaying the obligatory fox mask or two on the walls, a fox's rear quarters (or whatever the opposite of mask may be) stick out from the wall of the narrow passageway. As well as hunting and fell running connections there are also lead mining connections. One of the biggest of the old lead mines, Gategill, used to be worked just a stones throw from the village centre; as if in memory of this a display cabinet beside the fireplace houses a good collection of minerals, some of which have local origins. At the rear of the pub is a quiet patio with a few tables, a nice place to sit on a summers afternoon with good views over the fells to the south. The pub has a separate family room upstairs. Hours of opening for both pubs tend to be 11am-3pm and 6pm-11pm, possibly longer at summer weekends. Both pubs also do bar meals at lunchtime and early evenings.

The Walk

Pass the Horse and Farrier on your right and walk over the bridge across the beck. On your right here is a public footpath sign; follow the direction indicated, walk alongside the cottages and then bear right, following Kilnhow (or Blease) Beck upstream. The precipitous slopes of

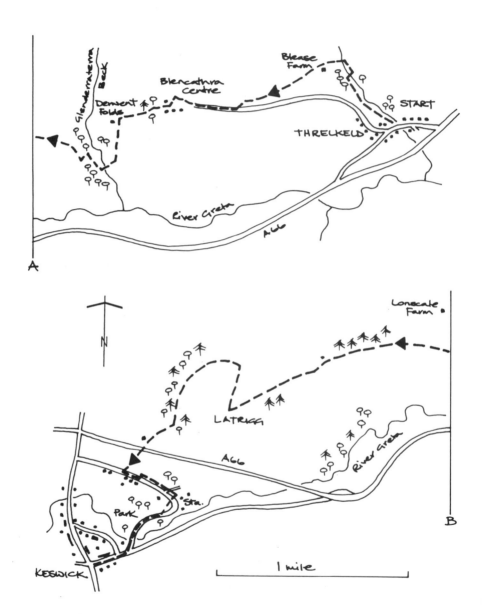

Blencathra rise almost from the back gardens of the huddles of cottages that comprise much of Threlkeld. Remain on the left hand bank until you reach the footbridge (not the first one you'll see but the one the path leads directly to), cross this and carry on up through the dell. Recross the beck, walk up through the car park and up the path beyond, signposted (on the wall) for Blease and Blencathra.

Some way upstream a footbridge crosses the beck below a fine waterfall, the most boisterous of a long series of shoots, falls and rapids. Climb the flight of steps, a grand view opening out, right, to Great and Little Mell Fells and the high Pennine Fells of Melmerby and Knock. Keep your eyes peeled for the path angling down to the left to cross the beck (an easy stride) above another torrent. Beyond this, climb the stile, keep the wall on your left, and walk to Blease Farm. Go to the right of the stables, the first buildings you reach, and walk behind the farm. Continue across the line of stiles and keep the subsequent wall on your left.

There's a fine view down St. John's in the Vale to your left, leading to the heights of Helvellyn in the distance. Keep the wall on your left and tackle a series of gates, stiles and a footbridge, eventually passing some sheep pens to join a minor road. Continue straight ahead along this until the road angles left to the Blencathra Centre. At this point go straight ahead along the rough road signposted to the Centre's car park. When you reach the cattle grid go through the gate on the left and walk on through the trees to the driveway, turning right along this and winding a way past the barns, offices and chalets that comprise the Blencathra Centre. This used to be an isolation hospital where those with "infectious diseases" were confined; nowadays it is the northern base of the Lake District Special Planning Board and a centre for self catering holidays.

At the far end of the buildings follow the footpath sign for Keswick and walk along the narrow fenced path. Once through the gate at the far end bear left and walk down to the gate leading to a path through the fir plantation. Bear half right at the end and walk towards the white cottage in the distance, soon joining the lane which leads up to this. Immediately before the cottage, Derwentfolds, turn left at the sign for Keswick and Skiddaw, then following this ancient trackway down to the worn old wooden footbridge over the Glenderaterra Beck. Walk up the winding track beyond and, on reaching the wider roadway at the top, turn right and walk uphill with this.

Views now open out to your left across the top end of Keswick and along the length of the Newlands Valley to the high peaks above Buttermere and, further to the left, the bulk of Great Gable. When the track splits go left and then right over the stile at the sign for Skiddaw. Once over the stile go left up the obvious path that climbs steeply up through the area of gorse bushes. At the top of this favour your right hand slightly to find a field track that strikes up along the long snout of the hillside ahead. Up to your right the great bare flanks of Lonscale Fell mark the eastern edge of the Skiddaw range, the obvious, wide path up Skiddaw itself scours its way up the fellside slightly further westwards.

Remain with the well worn path and walk up alongside but above the fir plantation on your right. Pass through the gap in the wall beside the old sheep pen and then bear half left up the hillside. When you strike across the line of an old field road bear right along this and climb gradually up the hillside with it. This track hugs the top edge of a series of small scars and eventually brings you to a stile over a wall, beyond which the path levels out along the ridge leading to the top of Latrigg. This is one of the classic low-level views in the Lake District. Keswick is spread at your feet, beyond which is Derwentwater and the mountains guarding Scafell, the highest of England's mountains at 3210 feet. To the northwest is Bassenthwaite Lake, way beyond this the Solway Firth glistens and, beyond this, the mountains of Dumfries and Galloway form the horizon.

There are a number of paths leading down from Latrigg. The easiest one to follow goes to the right just behind the bench, placed near the summit in 1991 in memory of an aged resident of Keswick. The path is an obvious terrace leading north steadily down the fellside. The bulk of Skiddaw is straight ahead; when bathed in the late afternoon sun it is a riot of colours, nothing like the monotonous slate grey it so often appears from Keswick. Cross the top of a couple of becks, the second on a short stretch of boardwalk. About 150 yards beyond this bear left off the main path and drop steeply down along the path through the bracken to reach a wider path at the bottom. Turn left along this and walk along to the woods.

Remain with the path which traces the edge of the woods and will eventually bring you to a bridge across the A66 Keswick by-pass. At the end of the lane cross the road and turn left. When the footpath runs out recross the road and walk along the footpath behind the hedge. Cross directly over the minor road at the end and walk along a further stretch of path behind a hedge. When you see the modernist swimming pool on your right, cross the road to it and walk alongside to find Station Road which leads down to central Keswick.

One of the classic low–level views in the Lake District, here of Blease Fell and Great Mell Fell, is from Latrigg

6. Mungrisdale

Route: Scales – Southerfell – Mungrisdale – Bannerdale – Mousthwaite Comb

Distance: 7.5 miles

Start: The White Horse Inn, Scales. Grid reference: NY 343269

Map: O.S. Outdoor Leisure Series Sheet 5, The English Lakes NE

Access: Scales is a farm, a couple of houses and a pub on the A66 road about five miles east of Keswick. The White Horse is well signposted to the left off the main road on a part of the old main road now left as a backwater by road improvements.

The White Horse (07687 79241)

The low, white painted pub lies at the break of slope where the heights of Blencathra give way to the gentle pastures beside the lower reaches of the Glenderamackin river. Behind the pub the bracken and bilberry clothed slopes of Scales Fell rise precipitously to over 2000 feet, a further, massive cliff taking the summit of Blencathra to 2847 feet, one of the highest in The Lake District. From the terrace in front the extensive views beyond the barn sweep across Matterdale Common to Great Dodd, Stybarrow Dodd and Helvellyn whilst off to the right the Derwent Fells take the eye towards Great Gable and the Scafell group. Small wonder, then, that this is a very popular place of refreshment for ramblers of the armchair school.

The White Horse is now a free house, having been tied for many years to Jennings. Marstons is now the order of the day at the small bar, both the excellent Pedigree and Burton Bitter being available on handpump. The open plan bar is based around a massive central fireplace and chimneybreast, another small fire adjoins the bar. Two small rooms are set of from this main area, the one beside the bar was, until recently, the old dairy of the farm the pub once was. It's about 300 years old, the solid, blackened beams within testimony to its years of service. These beams support a mixture of brasses and a trailing hop-vine.

The White Horse, Scales: armchair ramblers enjoy sweeping views of the fells from the terrace.

The walls sport prints, photographs and jocular cartoons of the local Blencathra Hunt which is based nearby and meets at the pub each November; one victim of this practice stands beside the main fireplace. Other unfortunate creatures include a stuffed owl, a pine marten and a large otter, killed by a car in the North Pennines and given, freshly run over, to the landlord; he put it in the deep freeze at the local kennels until a suitable taxidermist could be contacted! The deep window-sills and many shelves are covered in a veritable jungle of potted plants and flowers, outside are glorious window-boxes.

The pub has a good reputation for the quality and quantity of bar meals which can be sampled between 12 noon and 1.45pm, 7-8.30pm (summer), lunchtimes and weekend evenings only in winter. Pub hours are 11.30am- 3pm and 6-11pm.

The Walk

Turn left from the pub and within a few paces bear left at the fork, walking up along the road which is, as the old sign suggests, gated. You remain with this narrow back road for about three miles, climbing gradually above and away from the main A66. The lone, conical hill sticking out of the wide valley is Great Mell Fell. In a mile or so the lane sweeps northwards up along the peaceful valley of the River Glenderamackin. Up to your left the broad sweep of Souther Fell is one of the family of fells which mark the north-eastern end of the peaks of the Lake District. To your right, beyond the broad valley of the Glenderamackin, the modest crags and rough pastures are the western edge of Greystoke Park, a huge manor house and vast private estate belonging to the Howard Family, Dukes of Norfolk, and said to be the largest single tract of land in England not crossed by a public footpath or right of way. It was used as a base and training area by the Polish army during the second war but, since then, access has been jealously guarded.

After passing by several farms (including Southerfell Farm and Cottage, a riot of colour in summer when virtually submerged beneath window boxes and hanging baskets) the lane reaches the hamlet of Mungrisdale, passing behind the Mill Inn (Theakstons and Hesket Newmarket beers, bar snacks) and across the river to reach a junction. Turn left here and walk the few yards to the rough lane on your left, marked by a telephone box and a footpath sign for Mungrisdale Common. This is the route you should follow, but its worth taking a few minutes to walk the extra few hundred yards along the "main" road to find the tiny church of St. Kentigern, dating from 1726 and housing a lovely, stretched, three decker pulpit. The name Mungrisdale is a derivation of "St. Mungo's Valley of the Pigs," St. Mungo being another name for St. Kentigern, an Eighth Century Bishop of Glasgow.

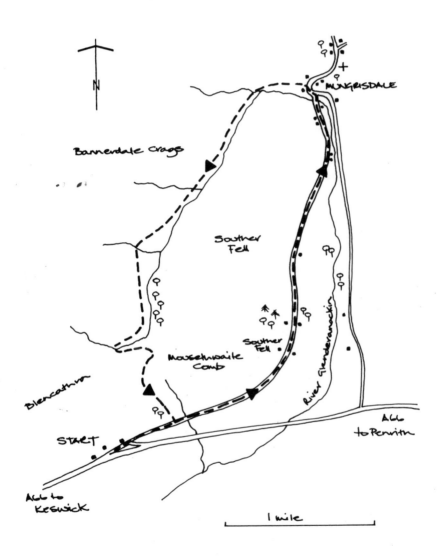

N

Bannerdale Crags

MUNGRISDALE

Souther Fell

Souther Fell

Mousethwaite Comb

River Glenderamackin

Blencathra

START

A66 to Penrith

A66 to Keswick

1 mile

Back to the telephone box, walk up the rough road past Bannerdale Cottage and through the gate leading out into unenclosed land. This is a very bare, austere part of the Lakes, a series of great whaleback fells separated by lonely valleys, sharp crags and rough scree slopes; it's unlikely you'll see more than a couple of walkers for the next three or four miles. Walk on ahead up the track, cross the footbridge beside the ford and walk a few paces beyond. Here bear left off the main track and walk up the narrow path running along a ridge just above the Glenderamackin. In a while this widens to become an obvious path through the bracken, a path you should follow all the way up the valley.

On the left the steep western slope of Souther Fell is a constant companion, its features pock-marked in areas where ephemeral springs have caused small areas of hillside to slump. To your right are impressive views up several side valleys to the heights of Bannerdale Crags – Bannerdale is the first of the valleys – which mark a sudden end to the high plateau of Mungrisdale Common. This area is still important for sheep grazing but was once host to gangs of lead miners toiling to win the precious ore from small mines and adits driven into the inhospitable mountainsides; the track you are following is an old miner's track leading down from old workings near Scales Tarn, beneath Blencathra.

In this valley in 1744 occurred one of the great unexplained mysteries of England. A spectral army of mounted and footsoldiers, cannon and waggons, passed silently down the valley towards distant Carlisle, a passing witnessed over several hours by tens of local people who later made dispositions with the local rector to this effect. This mass sighting remains a mystery to this day, mass hallucination, perhaps. At the time the event was taken as a harbinger that Charles Edward's (Bonnie Prince Charlie) campaign to reclaim the throne would fail – which it did a year later.

Ford Bannerdale Beck and continue up the main valley, the path gradually climbing away from the Glenderamackin to ford a second side stream some few hundred yards up a side valley. Look back from this point for extensive views out of the narrow main valley and across to the distant Pennines. The path heads back towards the Glenderamackin, still gaining height all the time. At one point look out for one of the slabs of rock which lie across a side stream, it looks for all the world as if someone wearing a size seven left boot had stood as the rock formed to leave a deep, everlasting impression in these Skiddaw Slates (perhaps a ghostly footsoldier...). Eventually the path and river swing right (west) around the snout of White Horse Bent. Soon after this bear left down a narrow path to reach a wide wooden plank bridge over the river, beyond which start the short, steady climb up to the watershed. As you walk up this slope allow an occasional look behind for ever-better views of the very distinct summit of Blencathra, its shape explaining the alternative name, Saddleback, of this mountain.

The haunted valley, Glenderamackin: dare you walk it alone?

In a short while you'll get to a bwlch (pass) and sudden extensive views to the south. The coombe immediately below is Mousthwaite Comb, the way back down to Scales. In the distance an old railway viaduct strides across the foot of an oak-tree filled valley, contrasting sharply with the regimented masses of the conifer plantations which creep over large areas of Matterdale Common. Beyond this the summits include, to the left, Place Fell and Loadpot Hill above Ullswater, High Street and the graceful curve of Helvellyn.

You need to descend the right hand side (as you look at it) of Mousthwaite Comb so look for the path which will take you from the bwlch fairly steeply downwards. Part of the way down is a small spoil heap below a hole in the hillside, another reminder of the miners of days past. Simply remain with the path which eventually meets the corner of a fence. Go round to the left of this and continue downhill, the fence on your right. Walk across several stretches of boardwalk and work down to the surfaced lane, turning right along this to return to The White Horse about half a mile away.

The hamlet of Mungrisdale, with Bannerdale Crags behind.

7. Crummock Water

Route: Loweswater – Mosedale – Scale Force – Crummock Water

Distance: 7 miles

Map: O.S. Outdoor Leisure Series Sheet 4, The English Lakes NW

Start: The Kirkstile Inn, Loweswater. Grid reference: NY 142208

Access: Loweswater village is about eight miles south of Cockermouth and about a mile east of Loweswater, the lake. From Cockermouth take the B5292 road towards Buttermere, go through Low Lorton and then follow the signs for Loweswater. The Kirkstile Inn is opposite the village church and is signposted from the road beside the red telephone box, about half a mile past the Scale Hill Hotel.

The Kirkstile Inn (090085 219)

There's not much to Loweswater except a church, a pub and a scattering of farms and cottages. The Inn has, over the years, gradually taken over parts of the farm it was once a part of and is now a sizeable concern. The olde-world interior reflects its past life as a farm, with harnesses, bits, yokes and a branding iron filling the shelves, nooks, crannies and walls. A series of old photographs mounted on the whitewashed and bare stone walls shows the Inn and village as it was. Near the bar is a small display of minerals and semi-precious stones to be found locally whilst behind the bar is an enormous brass(?) horn. It's a good job that last orders aren't signalled by a blast on this...

A jumble of wall benches and pews provide the main seating in both the upper and lower rooms, the latter also hosts a piano; in winter there's a good log fire. There's a separate family and games room in one of the adjoining old barns. At the front of the pub the large lawn is dotted with tables, undoubtedly the best place from which to appreciate the stunning views across the shallow valley of Park Beck to White Crag, the steep north end of Mellbreak Fell which runs the length of the western side of Crummock Water. Jennings's Bitter is the beer on offer at the one bar, there's also an extensive range of bar meals.

The Walk

(Except in very dry weather, a short section of this walk will be very boggy).

Walk down beside the pub and bear right along the "No Through Road" which runs along the foot of the garden. Cross the beck and walk on, soon passing the white-painted Kirkhead Farm. Stay with the road, by now a roughly surfaced track, and wind very gradually uphill between the thick stone walls. On your left are glimpses to the bottom end of Crummock Water, soon disappearing behind the great wall that is Mellbreak. Go through the gate at the end and bear slightly right, continuing along the track with a wall to your right. In a short while you'll get a good view, right, up Loweswater before this, too, is hidden from view by a steep sided Fell, Little Dodd.

This is an old miners' track leading to some long-abandoned workings on the western flank of lonely Mosedale, a track you follow for a mile or so. It's as lonely a place as you'll find anywhere in the Lakes, the steep flanks of Mellbreak on your left and Hen Comb to your right scarred with crags and screes haunted by jackdaws and buzzard. Eventually, the fence on your right swings right and cuts across the widening valley of Mosedale Beck. Just before this point a path angles up to the left and away from the miners track, gradually gaining height to pass about fifty yards behind the only tree you'll see in this wild valley.

Take this path and follow it behind the tree and then virtually along the contour around the hillside. Ahead is the long fellside of Gale Fell rising steeply beyond the wide, shallow bowl which is the top end of Mosedale, once a busy junction of pack horse routes between the coastal ports at Workington, Whitehaven and Maryport and the inland towns of the Lake District. These hauliers worked day and night, the vision of lamps carried by the jagger or on the leading pony, bobbing through such high passes on a dark night or strung along hillsides like fireflies is an evocation of pre-Victorian England hard to match.

A short distance after passing by an isolated old gate and gateposts, the path bears round to the left and passes around the southern end of Mellbreak. At this point leave the obvious path and go straight ahead,

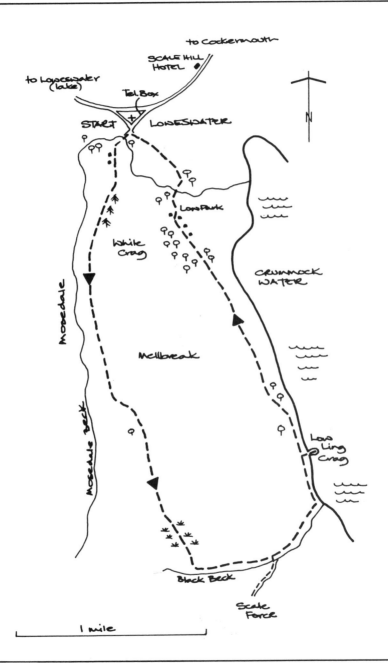

to Cockermouth

SCALE HILL
HOTEL

to Loweswater
(lake)

Tel. Box

START

LOWESWATER

N

Lowpark

White
Crag

CRUMMOCK
WATER

Mosedale

Melbreak

Mosedale Beck

Low
Ling
Crag

Black Beck

Scale
Force

1 mile

walking across the wide, flattened area of marsh grass and past an isolated pole. It may be very boggy underfoot here but persevere, this is the right of way rather than the dry one which swung away to the left! Just aim for the sharp, wooded cleft cut into the side of Gale Fell ahead.

At the far end of this marshy section you'll reach a fence crossed by two stiles. Climb the left hand one and then follow the line of the fence to your right, falling steeply for a short distance towards the narrow Black Beck. Before you reach the beck turn left and walk down the path on this left hand side of the beck, views over the southern end of Crummock Water gradually opening out.

Your next target is the wooded defile on the far side of the valley. As you get to a point opposite this look down into the valley to locate a footbridge and work your way down to this; there is no obvious, well trodden path so just take the easiest line. Once across this follow the path up the right side of the stream to reach the defile, cut over thousands of years by the narrow waterfall of Scale Force. This is one of the highest single falls in England, gushing well over one hundred feet into the tree-covered gorge. Clamber up to the plunge pool at the foot of the fall to fully appreciate it, here you'll probably find members of the British Ovine High Diving Team floating around. Even this precipitous landscape didn't escape the attentions of doughty miners in years past, the very red, thin soil and scree to the left of the fall is eroded from an adit opened up to mine small quantities of iron ore.

Retrace your steps to the footbridge (the one across Black Beck, not the one at the foot of the waterfall), cross it and turn right down the narrow path, following this down to the lake shore of Crummock Water. Walk up along this western shore, taking opportunity in a short while to walk out onto the promontory of Low Ling Crag from where are superb views south to Fleetwith Pike and Haystacks, beyond the top end of hidden Buttermere.

Continue northwards along the shore, cross through the line of the old wall and walk to the point where slabs of rock come down to the shore. Once across these slabs angle slightly left away from the lakeside path and climb very gradually uphill. At first there's no obvious path, it's simply a matter of picking your way through the bracken and across several boggy areas but in the end an obvious path develops around the contour just a stone's throw above the lakeside path.

Scale Force: this narrow waterfall drops more than one hundred feet to the gorge it has cut over thousands of years.

By the time you reach the bottom end of the lake this upper path is one hundred or so yards above the lower one. Join the line of the wall on your right and follow this, shortly entering the edge of an old oakwood. The path winds through this and behind a couple of farmhouses, just beyond the second of these pass through the gate and walk along the walled bridleway to Lowpark. Bear slightly left at the end of the bridleway and pass by Garth Cottage on your left. At the end of the drive turn left along the surfaced road, cross the bridge and turn left again at the junction to return to the Kirkstile Inn in about a quarter of a mile.

8. Borrowdale

Route: Rosthwaite – Castle Crag – Johnny's Wood

Distance: 4.5 miles

Map: O.S. Outdoor Leisure Series Sheet 4, The English Lakes NW

Start: The Riverside Bar, Rosthwaite. Grid reference: NY 259148

Access: Rosthwaite is a small village in Borrowdale about three miles south of Derwentwater on the road from Keswick to the Honister Pass. The Riverside Bar is at the rear of The Scafell Hotel in the village centre. Park in the village car park, the entrance to which is opposite the village shop.

The Riverside Bar (07687 77208)

This must be one of the more unappealing entrances to a pub in the Lake District, alongside the concreted service road to the rear of the Scafell Hotel and through a door reminiscent of the exit of a cinema. Once past these trials, however, you're in a basic bar dedicated to walkers, ramblers and climbers, where evidence of participation in one of these pursuits is *de rigueur* and the furnishings as spartan as the fellsides that hem in the village – but who needs carpet and chintzy lampshades when you're more than a little damp and in search of succour?

On offer here are excellently kept Theakston's Best Bitter, XB and Old Peculier, accompanied by a range of bar snacks at lunch and early evening. If there's room base yourself on the slate terrace off the bar, built virtually above Stonethwaite Beck and with glorious views up to the heights of Brund Fell and Great Crag opposite. Hanging baskets trail nasturtiums into the Beck which is patrolled by kingfishers and dippers, keep an eye out, too, for woodpeckers and sparrow-hawks.

The Walk

Cross directly over the road and walk along the narrow road, signposted as a "Private Road," opposite the Scafell Hotel. Follow this lane up through the jumble of old barns, cottages and farms and bear right at the yew tree. Pass Yew Tree Farm to your left and follow the rough track beyond; remaining with this until you've crossed the old pack horse bridge across the River Derwent.

Turn right and follow the river downstream for a few hundred yards, then bear left with the main path through the area of rather scrubby oak and ash woodland. At the far side of this go over the stile beside the field gate and follow the obvious path up the steep hillside beyond, soon re-entering mixed deciduous woodland. A steep scramble brings you to a gate, once through which simply follow the well trodden path up to a ladder stile on the shoulder of the hill. Climb this and turn right, following the zig-zag path up the old slate tip to gain the summit of Castle Crag.

No obvious evidence of any fortification remains, the suspicion is that it's sharp edges, gullies and quarried faces were "romanticised" into a castle by writers and poets in times past although an old British fort has been recognised by authorities on this subject and the name "Borrow-dale" is derived from the Old English for "fort in the valley." The Crag was given to The National Trust in 1918 in memory of John Hamer, killed in the Great War along with other residents of Borrowdale, all remembered by a plaque at the summit. The old quarries on the Crag, together with others higher on High Spy were major employers in Borrowdale and for many people from Keswick; all are long abandoned even the large workings at the summit of the Honister Pass succumkbed some four years ago. The works of Sir Hugh Walpole, who lived in the valley, evoke these earlier days of the area.

The views from this isolated crag, a tooth in the so-called "Jaws of Borrowdale," are stunning. To the north is the length of Derwentwater, the distinctive peaks of Skiddaw looming at the far end. East, the lower fells of Grange and Watendlath and the wooded slopes of King's How make a dramatic foreground to the heights of Helvellyn which form the horizon. To the south are the more jagged summits of Glaramara and

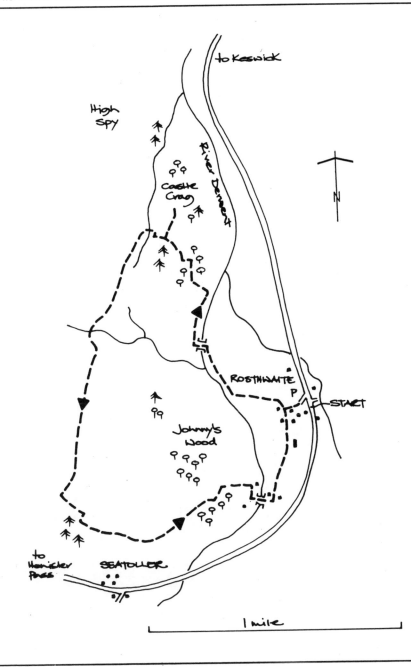

Interlocking fells drop precipitously to Broadslack Gill

Great End, Great Gable and Scafell, the jumbled mass of England's highest few acres. In the west the edge of High Spy plunges steeply down to the beautiful, gorge-like valley of Broadslack Gill, the route now followed by the walk.

Retrace your steps down the slate-waste tip to the ladder stile. Don't recross it but turn right and follow the path down beneath the trees. Ignore the ladder stile on your left in a few yards, instead walk along the line of the slate wall, then fence on your left. Climb the stile, descend the ladder stile beyond this and walk down the steep path to the valley bottom. Turn left and follow the old miners track upstream, the infant river on your left.

Within a few hundred yards you'll cross the watershed between Broadslack Gill and a smaller, unnamed brook. Remain with the track until you reach a large cairn of stones, here bearing left along the narrower path through the bracken, very gradually losing a little height. Cross the two footbridges beneath the birch tree and walk to the gate beyond. Once through this stick with the path, roughly following the line of a wall down to your left and heading for the bwlch, or pass, at the back of the tree-covered crag some distance ahead. Once through this shallow pass follow the line of the wall for a further 200 or so yards to reach two gates. Go through the left hand one of these.

Up to your right is the road leading up to the Honister Pass and down in the valley ahead the village of Seatoller. Follow the wide green path down from the gate and then join the track, following this gently downhill. Go through the kissing gate beside the second gate you reach and wind right with the track. Immediately before reaching the line of fir trees on your left, turn left off the track and walk down the field path through the bracken. Bear left beneath the ash and oak trees, go through the gate and follow either of the paths beyond to reach a further gate. Once through this follow the main track through the woods, an old broken wall on your right. This is Johnny's Wood, a National Trust woodland of sessile oak, sycamore and birch, renowned also for the variety of mosses, lichens, fungi and rare plants such as liverworts largely confined to such damp, old woodland areas.

Ignore the fork to the left and remain with the main path, eventually reaching a gap through the wall, beyond which the path goes steeply downhill to reach the edge of the woods. Cross the stile beyond the holly trees and turn right, walking along behind the barns to reach a gate. Once through this turn left and cross the old single arched bridge over the river. Walk up the surfaced road beyond this and turn left at the top, at the footpath sign in front of Peat How Barn. Go through the gate and follow the line of the wall on your right, passing through this at the far end of the pasture then walking towards the slate-built cottages. Climb the stile and walk along the field behind these cottages, go through the gate at the end, bear right and then turn left along the tarmaced lane, winding your way back through the cottages and barns to regain the main street at Rosthwaite.

Pause for contemplation at New Bridge, Dale Head

9. Gowbarrow

Route: Dockray – High Force – Yew Crag – Aira Force

Distance: 4.5 miles

Map: O.S. Outdoor Leisure Series Sheet 5, The English Lakes, NE.

Start: The Royal Hotel, Dockray. Grid reference: NY 393216.

Access: Follow the A592 road along the north/west shore of Ullswater to the junction with the A5091 signposted for Troutbeck. Take this road and follow it for about a mile and a half, the Royal Hotel is on the left at the hamlet of Dockray.

The Royal Hotel (07684 82356)

The Hotel stands alongside Aira Beck virtually surrounded by the high fells that sweep down to Ullswater, a situation best appreciated from the large beer garden, shaded by tall firs but offering glorious views to contemplate whilst sipping the Theakston's XB, Whitbread Trophy or Castle Eden on sale here. The solid, whitewashed building is a residential hotel, the guests tending to use the more comfortable of the two bars. The top bar is the one most popular with ramblers and is nearly always busy with groups resting en route to/from treks on nearby Watermillock Common or Gowbarrow, being open all day, 11-11. It's simply furnished with a few wall benches and tables, the beams hosting the odd ornament or two and the walls hung with cartoons and photo's of the local hunt. In winter a good woodburning fire adds to the atmosphere of one of the more welcoming of Lakeland's walkers pubs.

The Walk

(This walk includes a very steep downhill section down the face of a crag, not recommended for those with problem knees).

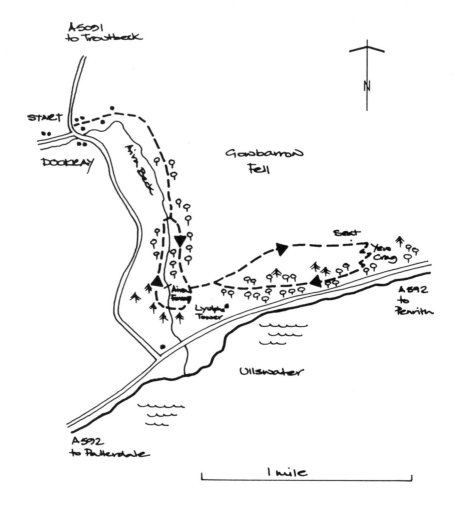

A5091
to Troutbeck

N

START

DOCKRAY

Aira Beck

Gowbarrow
Fell

Aira
Force

Lyulph's
Tower

Seat

Yew
Crag

A592
to
Penrith

Ullswater

A592
to Patterdale

1 mile

Cross the main road opposite the hotel and walk down the footpath signposted for Aira Force and Ulcat which wends its way to the right of the farm and row of cottages. Carry on down this rough driveway, ignoring the footpath to Ulcat that diverges to the left after a while. Virtually at the end of the drive pass between the cottage to your left and the barn, topped by a weather-vane shaped like a curlew, to your right, cross the sleeper bridge over the beck and bear right, following the path around the hillside.

Pass through the gate and continue ahead across the rough pasture. Already, extensive view ahead stretch to Martindale Common and Place Fell, to your left the craggy heights of Gowbarrow Fell, all of which is owned by The National Trust. You'll soon reach an area of patchy ash and birch woodland alongside the first of the long series of torrents and falls cut by Aira Beck as it plunges down to Ullswater, a mile or so away.

The path darts in and out of the woods and side paths go off to the right to various falls including High Force, a shadow of its namesake in the Yorkshire Dales but still well worth seeing. Follow the main path and views open out along the top end of Ullswater and the lower slopes of Helvellyn. You'll reach an open, bracken covered clearing, at the far side of which a kissing gate leads to a path through the trees and down to a pseudo-pack horse bridge, built in memory of one Stephen Edward Spring-Rice. Aira Force itself is directly below this bridge, better viewed on the return part of the walk.

Remain on the left hand side of the beck and follow the path back up the bank alongside a stretch of rail fencing. About two hundred yards will bring you to a split in the path. Go left here and pass through the gate, continuing along the obvious path beyond for a further two hundred or so yards. Down to your right is the curious building called Lyulph's Tower. The current building dates from the 1780's, built as a shooting lodge for the Howard Family, Dukes of Norfolk, who are big landowners in this part of the Lake District. Its foundations, however, are thought to be much earlier, based on a thirteenth century pele tower.

At the split in the path bear left and climb the increasingly steep path which cuts across this southern face of Gowbarrow Fell, a craggy hillside haunted by jackdaws, ravens and sparrow-hawks. On reaching the split in the path some yards directly above a wedge of trees take the right, lower path and follow this along to the top of Yew Crag, about a quarter of a mile further along. Just before the Crag is the Memorial Seat, one of many such in the mountains. This one is dedicated simply "A thanks offering, October 1905." Take the path which goes to the right here, passing immediately behind the summit of the Crag. From here is one of the classic views of Ullswater, south west along the lake to Patterdale and the ribs of Helvellyn, opposite are Sleet Fell, Place Fell and the heights of Martindale Common leading up to High Street.

Cross the stile you come to in a short distance and stick with the narrow but obvious path down through the heather. The path starts its steep, zig-zag descent of the face of Yew Crag. Don't be fooled by various side paths which just lead to viewpoints, just take it slowly and discern the main path which soon leads into scrubby oak woodland. At one or two points there are rough steps hewn or laid to aid the descent, but you never need to scramble on all fours; the first set of steps occurs just above some yew trees. You'll reach a point where the path swings sharp left at the foot of a rock face against which is set an old wooden fence. A few yards after this and just below a yew tree the path splits into three virtually alongside a large, whitened old tree stump. Take the right hand path here, walk by the stump and stick with this path as it gradually looses height. At one point the path crosses the top of a scree slope, a particularly narrow section.

Climb the stile and carry on along the path, ignoring any paths to left or right and gradually regaining a little height. Pass by another of the memorial seats at the top of a large clearing, giving a nice low-level view across the lake, and eventually the path comes out above Lyulph's Tower. Retrace your earlier steps for a few hundred yards until you can see the gate off to your right. Here bear left along the path to the little stile beneath a gnarled old beech tree. Beyond this join the main path and walk down to the footbridge across Aira Beck.

Cross this bridge and then bear right along the path which starts uphill beneath a canopy of yews, then mixed broadleaf and fir trees, some of the latter well over 150 feet high. This is all part of the National Trust's Aira Force Estate, one of the Trust's earliest properties in the Lakes dating from 1906. Down to your right the beck courses over a series of falls and shoots. At the point where a path comes in from the left through a kissing gate bear right and walk a few yards to some steps on your right. The route of the walk remains on this upper level, but take the opportunity to go some way down these steps to take benefit of the fine view of Aira Force, tumbling some sixty feet into a deep, boulder strewn defile clothed in ferns and mosses.

Return to the upper path and carry on upstream, soon reaching the stone bridge across the top of the Force. Remain on the near bank, however, and continue upstream alongside the Beck to reach a further footbridge at a spot where the water has seriously undercut the bank resulting in overhangs and pot holes. Cross this bridge, favour the left hand path at the far side and climb up the slope to find the main path. Bear left along this, the path the walk followed earlier in the walk, and walk the remaining mile back to Dockray.

Aira Force

Broad-leaved woodland enhances the pleasure of walking in this delightful area

Westmorland

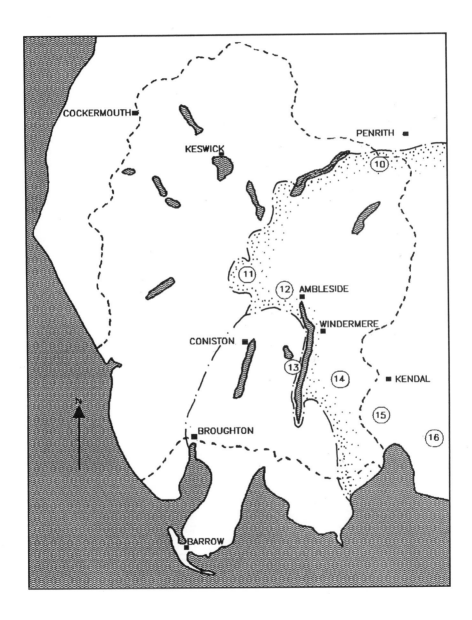

10. Askham

Route: Askham – Moor Divock – Helton – Whale

Distance: 8 miles

Map: O.S. Outdoor Leisure Series Sheet 5, The English Lakes NE.

Start: The Queen's Head, Askham. Grid Reference: NY 513237.

Access: Askham is four miles due south of Penrith. Take the A6 south from Penrith to Eamont Bridge, about 1.5 miles away. Almost immediately after crossing the traffic light-controlled bridge turn right along the B5320 towards Ullswater. In a mile or so take the road to the left signposted for Askham and Haweswater, Askham is about three miles along this road, the pub is on your left as you enter the village.

The Queen's Head (09312 225)

The old part of Askham is shaped rather like an egg-timer. Two enormous village greens form the bowls whilst the waist is the village square beside which stands The Queen's Head, a position it has occupied for several centuries having been a popular stopping point for trains of pack horses (or, at least, the jagger in charge of them..). Step inside and you can't but wonder if these beasts of burden were solely used to carry copper, if there's ever a world copper shortage then melting down the Queen's Head would alleviate it. Enormous copper (and brass) plates decorate the walls, burnished kettles weigh down the ceiling whilst jugs, pans and post horns decorate the dark oak beams, a central feature of the main front room. The bar top, too, is covered with rolled copper, two handpumps nestle at the far end, used to serve up Wards Bitter and Vaux Sampson.

A large old fireplace dominates one wall, probably dating from the foundation of the pub in 1672; nearby is a spice cupboard dated 1869. The pub evidently had past connections with a local pack of otter hounds; there are a few mounted otter masks dating from the 1930's and the sharp eyed will spot mounted otter paws (!) nailed to one of the beams, victims of this barbaric practice from Gowbarrow (west of Ullswater) in 1937.

There's another large room and bar at the back of the pub where "copper blindness" is less of a problem. Outside are a few benches and tables with views up the long upper green, there's also a large garden away from the quiet road. All in all, it's a very welcoming pub run by a landlady new to the area and in a village a million miles away from the hoards which can make the Lake District such a pain.

Askham

If Askham were nearer to Ambleside it would be as popular as Grasmere or Hawkshead, as it is the village retains it's tranquillity. The upper and lower village greens are pinched together at the waist by a couple of farms creating the possibility of making two large corrals, useful for detaining flocks of sheep herded down from the moorland pastures above the village before shearing or driving to market. Colourwashed seventeenth and eighteenth century cottages, yeomens houses and farms line these greens like a varnish as they tumble from the moors to the River Lowther. The Lords of the Manor, the Lonsdales, live in the medieval Askham Hall, just north of the lower, eastern green. They moved there in 1936 from Lowther Castle, a pseudo-Gothic mansion built for the family in 1811 by Robert Smirke, architect also of the British Museum. Now only the facade of the Castle remains beyond the woods east of the Lowther – you can see it from the walk. At the foot of the village's main street is the other village pub, the Punch Bowl, and beyond this St. Peter's Church, perched on a terrace above the river.

The Walk

Cross the road from the Queen's Head and walk up the upper green, half way up favouring the right hand fork marked with a "No through road" symbol. As with the lower green it is kept closely cropped, the beautifully tended cottage gardens alongside complement this and many of the cottages are smothered by climbing roses and honeysuckles. The short-lived Askham Beck trickles along the south side of this green,

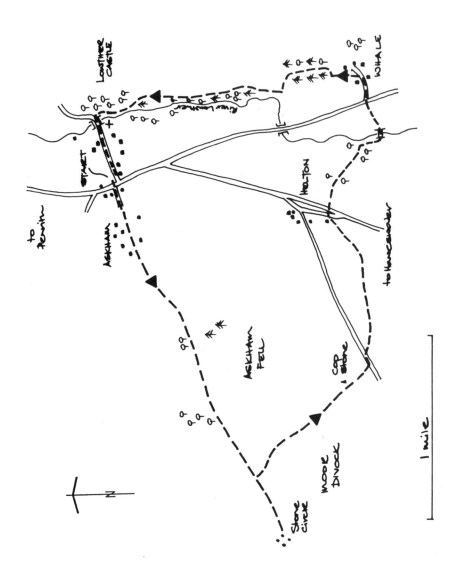

emerging from a spring just above the village and giving up the unequal struggle on the largely limestone rocks half way down this upper green.

The green narrows at the top end, known as Town End. Cross the cattle grid and follow the road for a few yards, then favour the rough field road which parallels the wall on your right, gradually climbing towards the moors. Stick with this, pass by the isolated barn and continue towards the copse on the hillside ahead. That this is limestone country is obviated by the solid limestone bloc walls and the outcrops of the light coloured rock forming sinuous lines through the moorland pastures.

Pass through the gate and continue with the copse of sycamore on your right. At this gate pause to look back to enjoy a long view across Askham, the turrets of Lowther Castle and the Lowther valley to the fortress-like heights of the north Pennines. Ahead and to your left, an extensive view over the moorlands opens out. Askham Fell and Moor Divock are the foreground, beyond these various higher summits culminate in Loadpot Hill, 2201 feet high.

Remain with the moorland road as it meanders over the sheep-cropped grassland, aiming for the left hand side of the straggle of woodland which marks the highest point of this part of the Fell. Just before reaching this a well used bridleway strikes across your path, you should bear left along this and follow it towards the higher ground in the distance. In about a half-mile an isolated signpost sticks up from the somewhat boggy moorland. This marks a crossing of bridleways, a glance to your right will reveal some cottages above Pooley Bridge at the top end of Ullswater, although the lake itself is not visible. You're now in rather Dartmoor-like landscape, wide, shallow valleys filled with bracken and flushes of boggy, reedy mires, interspersed with higher ridges of land, sudden sharp crags and liberally dotted with neolithic remains.

One of these remains is the next target so walk ahead from the signpost following the vaguely discernible bridleway towards Howtown. Pick your way through several flushes to arrive, a little over a quarter of a mile later, at a stone circle known as The Cockpit. Kept free of the encroaching bracken, this impressive monument stands beside the Roman Road known as High Street, nowadays kept well delineated by the boots and hooves of walkers and ponies. Listen out for the melancholic call of the curlew and the whirring sound of a sandpiper's wings as it is disturbed from feeding at one of the mires.

Retrace your steps to the isolated signpost and turn right, heading for Helton along the wide bridleway. On your right in a couple of hundred yards is an area of large shake holes, some of them over twenty feet deep. Shake holes are diagnostic features of limestone areas, formed when the land surface gradually sinks into areas where the limestone has been dissolved away by the action of rainwater at spots which are particularly well fissured. This particular area of shake holes is known as the Pulpit Holes, possibly so-named after meetings held there by Quakers in the Seventeenth century when their beliefs were frowned upon and the established church was openly hostile to them.

Continue along the bridleway, on both sides of which are a number of cairns, standing stones, stone circles and stone avenues, most difficult to see beneath the sea of bracken but nonetheless making this area, Moor Divock, an important one for the study of bronze age people and life. What is obvious, ahead, though, is a standing stone known as the Cop Stone. Excavations reveal that this stands at the centre of a low circular earth bank, it's purpose remains yet another mystery left by neolithic man. Continue past this and along the bridleway to reach the minor road a short distance later. There's a grand view up the Lowther valley from this point, coming in from the right is Heltondale Beck, draining the slopes of Helton Fell and Loadpot Hill.

Turn left along this minor road and about a hundred yards along bear right at the footpath sign, forcing a way through the high bracken. Within a few yards a ladder stile comes into view ahead, walk to this and enter the field beyond. Walk on down this long field aiming to reach the bottom left hand corner. Go through the gate here and walk ahead down the field to the gate at the bottom. This is one of a large number of long, narrow fields around Askham and Helton, a survival of medieval field systems that have long disappeared from most areas of England.

Once through the gate at the bottom walk along the walled track past the ash trees. Just past the second tree look carefully for the narrow gap stile on your left, go through this and walk diagonally across the pasture to the far bottom corner. Climb the stile and bear left, going through the gate beside the aluminium water trough. Head slightly right across this next field to the ladder stile at the far side and climb this. An obvious bank strikes down the length of the subsequent field, walk along the line of the bottom of this down to a stile giving access to a minor road at the edge of Helton.

Take a few minutes to explore this tiny village, at the top end of which is a large, rather unkempt green overlooked by a variety of cottages and villas. The one village street has many squat cottages dating from the 1600's and there's also a village pub, The Helton Inn, selling Theakstons to thirsting walkers. Return almost to the spot where you climbed the stile out of the last field and turn left down the track between the white painted cottage and the renovated barn. Cross straight over the road at the end and go along the narrow bridleway opposite, signposted for Whale.

This bridleway is a riot of colours during summer months. Dog roses, hawkweed, vetch, knapweed, woundwort, campion, toadflax and burdock to name but a few line and tumble across this ancient routeway. Remain with it virtually to its end, twenty yards or so before which you reach a point where there are gates to your left and right. Go through the left hand one, partially blocked by a low hawthorn tree, and walk ahead for a few yards towards a stile at the far side. Before you reach this you'll find a waymark post in the middle of the field directing you right. Climb the stile beneath the tree and cross the plank footbridge, then walk ahead to the substantial footbridge across the river Lowther. From this bridge on sunny days you'll see lots of trout in this crystal clear river, look out too for the flash of a kingfisher hunting its territory.

Once across the bridge bear right, pass through the bridleway gate and then turn left, following the line of wall up to the gate at the top. Cross straight over the minor road here and walk up the surfaced lane to the tiny hamlet of Whale. This is no more than half a dozen old farmhouses surrounding a little green, each house with a barn still attached, most of which seem still to function as such. The path you want is on the left just as you reach the green, immediately beyond the house with green-painted window surrounds. A public footpath sign points the way over a stone step stile. Walk through the garden and under the vast sycamore tree, keeping the wall on your right. Pass through the little gate at the top of the steps and walk ahead, leaving the wall to sweep away to Whale Farm.

Aim for the near corner of the woodland ahead, then look for the small stile giving access to these woods about twenty yards from this corner. Walk ahead into the woods for a couple of yards and turn left, following the track just inside the woods. It seems local practice simply to follow this track to the far end of the woods, pass through the gate and continue along the track. This isn't the official public right of way, however. To follow this, in a short while climb up to the obvious terrace and bear left along this, then following the rough path along to the far end of the woods. Look to your right to spot the stile out of the trees, then bear half left and walk down to the substantial stile at the foot of the field beside the river. Once over this turn right and follow the field road to and then alongside the plantation, passing through gates as necessary. This is all part of the Lowther Estate, this particular section marked as a deer park, although I didn't spot any.

At the far end of the plantation go through the gate and follow the track across the pasture, soon going through another gate and into the woods. Down to the left the Lowther courses its way over rapids and through a gorge cut into the sandstone. In about 150 yards a path diverges to the left, leaving the roadway to climb on through the trees to reach Lowther Castle. Take this narrow path and follow it through the fir, then deciduous, woodland high above the river. Eventually you'll reach a road at a bridge over the river, turn left here and walk up back into Askham, passing the church and walking through the lower green to return to the Queen's Head. Looking downstream from the bridge, the remains of the old weir are still obvious and buildings associated with the old village mill survive on the western bank.

11. Langdale Valleys

Route: Elterwater – Skelwith Bridge – Stang End – Little Langdale

Distance: 6 miles

Map: O.S. Outdoor Leisure Series Sheet 7 : The English Lakes, SE.

Start: The Britannia Inn, Elterwater. Grid Reference: NY 327048.

Access: Elterwater village is about four miles west of Ambleside. Take the A593 road for Coniston and fork right onto the B5343 in Skelwith Bridge, immediately before the Skelwith Bridge Hotel. Elterwater is signposted off this road about two miles further on. There is a car park in the village and a further one on the common beside the B5343.

The Britannia Inn (09667 210)

Narrow roads winding down from the Common and up from the Great Langdale Beck meet at the compact village green, dominated by an enormous maple tree and grazed by indolent sheep. An old village farmhouse and adjoining cobblers shop face one side of the green; dating back to Shakespeare's time they together now trade as The Britannia Inn.

At an indeterminate date, but certainly before 1875, the farmer supplemented his income by brewing ale for sale to quarry workers and agricultural labourers. By 1900 the farming side of his business was forgotten, the premises extended into the old cobblers shop and the pub was in business. The origin of the name is open to conjecture, well into the present century it was listed in trades directories simply as an "Ale House." Various other parts of the current pub once had other functions; the lounge area was a stable block whilst the back bar and parts of the adjoining staff accommodation were the village ballroom (essentially a general function room used for occasional dancing rather than one solely dedicated for use by exponents of the Rogers and Astaire school of movement).

These variations of use, together with limited cosmetic surgery, have resulted in a watering hole which is renowned far beyond the confines of the Lakes but one which retains its character even in the most

crowded of summers and supports a dedicated band of locals. There are
two bars, which comes as a surprise to even regular visitors. The main
bar is little more than a snug with a bar along the far wall separating the
public area from the kitchens and the ground-level "cellar." With barely
enough room to swing that proverbial cat and beams low enough to
trouble anyone who is too tall to make commercial airline cabin staff
status, the tiny room is all but filled by an enormous settle, a couple of
wall and window seats and a smattering of tables and benches. The
colourwashed walls sport a minimal selection of drawings and prints of
local scenes; the centre-piece is a large slate fireplace, host to a
welcoming and necessary log fire during the long winter months.

The Britannia Inn, Elterwater: the buildings, dating from Shakespearean Times,
face the traditional village green

There's nearly as much room to sit in the hallway which separates the
bar from the dining room and lounge, dedicated for the use of residents.
Outside is a large area of slate terracing resplendent with an array of
tables, benches and chairs offering a diverse prospect down the Brathay

Valley and to the surrounding heights and Fells. The other, tiny back bar is hidden in behind the pub. The main difference is that it has a solid slate floor rather than a carpet. Thus the main bar is dedicated to those walkers (and other customers) whose association with a mire or beck is by chance or misfortune, the back bar to those who delight in quagmire leaping as a serious undertaking.

The beers are Marston's Pedigree, Mitchells Best Bitter, Jennings Bitter and Dark Mild, all kept well enough to make even the most dedicated walker consider hanging up their boots for the duration. This duration is all day (11-11) every day (standard hours on Sundays) except for Christmas Day and Boxing Day. Bar meals are served from 12-2 and 6.30-9 and light bar snacks are available at most other times. Dogs and children are welcome; indeed, "We welcome everyone" enthused a member of the bar staff (who wishes to remain anonymous) "except mother-in-law."

Elterwater

The name both of the village and the nearby lake is held to be derived from the old Norse for "Swans Lake." It was probably these Scandinavian invaders who first settled the flat, boggy floor of the Langdale Valleys (the village lies square in the jaws of the Great Langdale Valley) a millenium and more ago; a site near Fell Foot in Little Langdale has been tentatively suggested as the site of a local Viking parliament. Before this time the Romans passed through – the route between the Roman forts at Ravenglass, Hard Knott and Ambleside ran along Little Langdale – and before them Neolithic hunters obtained materials for use as weapons from a Stone Axe "Factory" high on the Langdale Pikes, axes made from the volcanic tuff rocks here have been found throughout Britain.

The village remained an agricultural community, based largely on wool supplied to the emergent woollen centre of nearby Ambleside, until the 1750's when demand for the local green slate started to increase, resulting in the opening up of any number of small and large quarries in the surrounding hills. To quarry this ever growing amount of slate coarse gunpowder proved invaluable and a thriving gunpowder manufacturing industry became established towards the end of that Century, being fully licensed by the 1820s. One reason for this location was the plentiful supply of Juniper Trees locally, the wood of which makes excellent charcoal, a major base-ingredient of gunpowder. This survived until 1929 when nitro-glycerine finally became supreme. The site of the works is now developed as an exclusive timeshare facility, a suitable location, some might say, for such an explosive development issue to be sited...

Of the multitude of slate mines only one now remains open, employing perhaps seven people where once thousands would have toiled. With the loss of its industries the village did not die, it simply became a backwater and saw no expansion or development. Most of the houses are several centuries old; there are some fine old cottages down by Great Langdale Beck and some massive gunpowder or slate-money mansions hidden in the hillside woods beyond this, Elterwater Hall for example.

The Walk

Stroll downhill to the bridge over the Great Langdale Beck and walk into the car park on your side of the river. Half way along the park on the right a gate gives access to a riverside path; join this and walk downstream alongside the fast flowing water. In half a mile or so the path enters a small area of broadleaf woodland strewn with moss covered boulders. Remain with the main path through the trees, catching occasional glimpses of Elter Water beyond the fringing reedbeds on your right. On leaving the woods there is an exceptional view to your right across the lake to the twin peaks of the Langdale Pikes, some of Lakelands most immediately recognisable mountains.

Walk ahead through the waterside meadows, Elter Water gradually narrowing to become once more the Beck. At the far end of the meadows the walk enters a further stretch of woodland, this time characterised by spruce and pine trees which clothe the sides of a gorge the river has gouged out of the rocks. Within a short distance the gorge culminates in a modest but powerful waterfall, Skelwith Force, below which the river becomes braided, creating numerous small wood-covered islets. The rock band at the lip of the falls has been utilised as a weir, channelling water

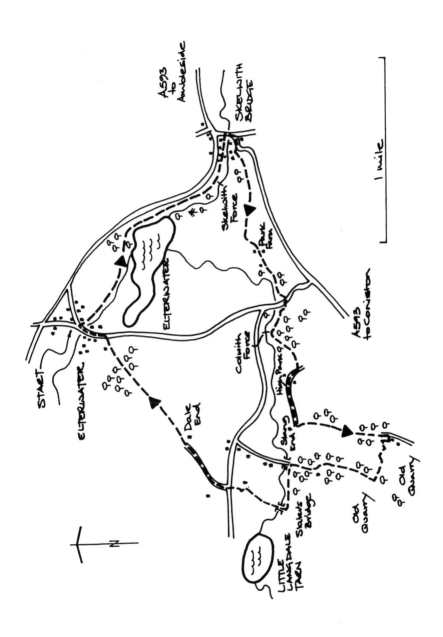

through a now-disused and broken pipe to the small stoneworks just above the bridge at Skelwith.

From the Force follow the riverside path down to these works and walk straight on through them, then following the service road down to the main A593. Cross the bridge and follow the road around the sharp right hand bend, then walk uphill for about 150 yards to find the public footpath sign on your right, pointing the way to Colwith Bridge. This path initially runs alongside a rough driveway before climbing gradually uphill through an area of woodland. Continue beyond the woods across the rough pastureland. Pass by the isolated farm, cross the brook and the stile and walk ahead to the gate at the bottom end of a small caravan site. Wind up through this, bear left and walk up to and through the farmyard at the top of the slope.

At the far side of the yard a footpath sign directs you between two buildings to the obvious path which crosses several pastures. A stile leads into a short, walled section, at the end of which go straight over the end of the driveway, through the kissing gate and angle left along the distinct path across the field. Enter the woods at the far side, which cloak the steep slopes above the Brathay, and follow the twisting path down to the small riverside pasture at the wood's foot. Walk upstream with the river to the stile giving access to the minor road.

Turn right and walk for less than 100 yards, keeping a sharp eye out to your left for a footpath sign, well hidden in the woodland edge, pointing up a few steps to a stile. Climb this and turn right, then following the path to and then upstream with the Brathay. The path is well braided so simply choose the one you can best manage. The various torrents and cataracts in the gorge culminate a few hundred yards upstream in Colwith Force, whose roar will have been your constant companion for the past few minutes. In a series of leaps the Brathay falls a good sixty feet into a deep, wooded defile. This natural "weir" has been put to good use in the past. A few squat buildings, black piping and precarious flights of wooden steps on the far side of the gorge mark an early supply of either water or hydro-electric power – from this distance it is impossible to make out. The feed to this leads in from a leat some yards above the top fall.

The path here leaves the river and angles up through the woodland. On reaching the top of the woods turn right, go through the gate and follow the waymark arrows to the huddle of buildings at High Park. Pass through the farmyard and walk along the narrow surfaced road beyond, contouring the slopes above the Little Langdale Valley and with Lingmoor Fell forming the far side. Ahead a sliver of tarmac climbs steeply up to the bwlch between Pike 'o Blisco and Wetherlam, this is the Wrynose Pass, one of Britain's steepest roads.

Walk along the road to reach the farm at Stang End and here take the broken-tarmac road, left, that goes up to the left of the barn. Remain with this, go through the gate into the woodlands and follow this roadway for the next half mile or so. Across the valley to your right, thick oak woods all but hide evidence of the slate mining that once was the lifeblood of the area, here and there shoulders of old waste heaps emerge from the greenwood. Virtually all the roads and trackways in this area are a result of this industry. Pass through a further gate and walk up through this area of National Trust woodlands along the wide bridleway.

At the end of the woods bear right at the fork, just before the stable building at the foot of the gardens of the impressive slate-built house on the crag top ahead. Wind down through the edge of the woods with this road to emerge on a wide plateau, the site of an old slate workings. The only remains are a few rusty hausers snaking through the undergrowth. Follow the track to the far edge, where this slate waste tip has encroached across a small valley. On the opposite side of this valley is a much larger old slate quarry. Follow the path along the middle one of the fingers of waste jutting out from the plateau you are on towards the far side of the valley, descend the steep but well defined path at its end and walk ahead up the slope to the foot of the far quarry slope. Here you'll find a rough old quarry road, turn right along this.

This next half mile is very pleasant walking along the old road, developed to serve old quarries and coppermines on the Tilberthwaite Fells. Nowadays it is a surprisingly quiet bridleway, the haunt of geologists and climbers seeking to challenge the slabs and faces left exposed by the miners of old. Passing by an isolated bungalow, the old road reaches the Brathay at a footbridge and ford. Cross neither, instead turn left along the narrow surfaced road and walk upstream. About 100 yards past the second gate which blocks this road look on your right for a gate and stile which lead to a path down to the river. Cross the river on the delightful little Slater Bridge, a narrow arch of slate worn and polished over the centuries by countless miners boots and pack horse hooves. To your left beyond the tree-capped knoll is Little Langdale Tarn.

Ignore the sign to Elterwater and walk up the narrow path ahead, keeping the wall to your right and walking up over several areas of bare rock. When you reach the farm track turn left along it and walk up to the minor road. Go left, then almost immediately right and up along the surfaced road marked as unsuitable for motor vehicles. Follow this past Dale End Farm and continue with it as it becomes a rough track. Off to your right are excellent views over to the crinkly ridge of Black Crag. Pass through the gate at the top and favour the right hand fork, walking down beside, then through, the woods. Off to the right you'll see Elter Water. Go straight ahead at the first junction and then left at the second, passing Elterwater Hall on your right and reaching the village at the bridge across the Beck.

12. Ambleside: Loughrigg

Route: Ambleside — Lily Tarn – Loughrigg Fell – Loughrigg Terrace – Rydal

Distance: 8 miles

Map: O.S. Outdoor Leisure Series Sheet 7, The English Lakes, SE.

Start: The Golden Rule, Ambleside. Grid Reference: NY 376046.

Access: Parking is very restricted at the pub. Instead, park in the (pay) car park at the northern end of Ambleside (off the A591 not far past the Bridge House). The Golden Rule is on the right a few yards up Smithy Brow, the road signposted for the Kirkstone Pass and virtually opposite the entrance to the car park.

The Golden Rule (05394 32257)

Many walkers will already know this old pub as perhaps the smallest and most convivial in Ambleside. In summer its almost hidden beneath hanging baskets and window boxes. It's an unpretentious place, simply furnished with cast iron tables, wall seats and the odd chair or stool. There's a small, rather dark side room used for darts and as a useful overspill, a tiny back yard with a few wooden tables that can, despite the proximity of other, higher buildings, be a bit of a sun trap, and a snug set down a few steps off the main room. This main room huddles up to the bar, behind which is displayed the artefact after which the place is named, a brass yard-measure. There's an open fire, wood panelling, a selection of foxes masks and a few brasses nailed to the low beams; the walls host prints and paintings of local scenes.

The beer is from Hartleys, a choice of the Mild, Bitter and XB all excellently kept by landlord John Lockley, although by the time you read this it's likely that the beer will be Robinsons from Stockport (a not unreasonable pint itself but sweeter than the local brew) or, even worse, Hartleys brewed at Stockport but still traded under the original name. Such is the lot of a landlord in the 1990's. The pub is deservedly popular

for its beers, its simple choice of bar snacks and welcoming atmosphere:
a favourite with locals and walkers alike and undisturbed by music.

Ambleside

The use of the local green-grey slate as the main building material for
the houses can give the town a very dour, foreboding look on a wet day,
a look relieved by its fine situation above the head of Windermere, and
at the meeting of major transport routes which ensures the town is
bustling, at least from Easter to the end of summer.

The site was first developed by the Romans who built a fort they called
Galava on a spit of land south west of today's town centre, just beyond
today's rugby club. The Romans colonised the area purely to exploit its
mineral resources and Ambleside doubtless acted as a transhipment
point for lead, copper and even gold mined in the surrounding fells, a
vital stop on the road they constructed through the Hard Knott Pass and
down to a port at Ravenglass on the west coast.

It was the woollen trade, however, that saw Ambleside develop as a
significant centre. The local Herdwick sheep produce an abundance of
wool which was valued far more highly in the Fifteenth to Seventeenth
Centuries than perhaps it is today. Most villages and hamlets could
boast spinning galleries and there was an enormous number of fulling
mills in the area (fulling being the process by which excess oils were
removed from the wool by washing, treating and beating the woollen
cloth) making use of the becks and streams to power fulling stocks.
Ambleside was the centre to which the partly finished product
gravitated for marketing and forwarding. The granting of its market
charter in 1650 confirmed Ambleside's status as a major player in this,
the single most important industry in England at the time.

The growth of the colonial cotton industry from about 1700 onwards
largely put paid to the woollen trade, however, and Ambleside suffered
a considerable decline. Echoes of the wool trade can still be seen,
however. The famous Bridge House was built as a folly-cum-summer
house for the estate of the now-demolished Ambleside Hall whose
owner made his fortune from wool. Spinning galleries can still be found
and Ambleside has its own water-wheel – albeit a replacement for an

earlier one – perched above Stock Ghyll beside an old woollen mill. Another survival from times gone by is the Rushbearing Ceremony held at St. Mary's Church on the third Saturday in July each year. The town has many ginnels, narrow back lanes and courtyards that repay a leisurely stroll around the compact centre, a lot more pleasant if done out of season.

The Walk

Walk down Smithy Brow to the main road and turn left. Cross the road and walk past the Bridge House towards the town centre. Bear right against the flow of traffic in the one way system, walking down Compston Road. About half way down the road bear right by the cinema at the sign to Rothay Park and Loughrigg and then immediately left along the road signposted as a dead end. This roadway continues alongside the churchyard and finishes by the junior school, beyond which is the Park. Walk ahead through the Park, beech hedge to your left, and cross the two footbridges at the far end.

On reaching the narrow road, turn right, cross the cattle grid and walk on for around fifty yards. Take the footpath and bridleway on the left, signposted to Loughrigg. Cross the cattle grid and wind up along this long driveway to the houses at the end. Here, hairpin sharp left in front of "High Barn" and walk up to the public footpath sign for Clappersgate. Go up through the woods, through a gap stile at the end and cross the brook beyond. A few yards further on, go right at the waymarked post and then right again in a few yards. Follow the obvious path which parallels the woodside wall some yards down to your right. Virtually at the far end, as the trees fade away to the right and the wall curves around in front of you, turn left and follow the main path up the fellside, a small crag on your left. Climb the ladder stile at the top and continue uphill to reach Lily Tarn a couple of hundred yards further on. True to its name it is, in summer, well dressed with large white water lilies.

Walk along the main path to the right of the tarn, soon passing two small pools. Go straight over a cross path and then join the line of a wall on your left; remain with the path alongside this and pass between sharp crags. Go through the wooden kissing gate and walk on through the

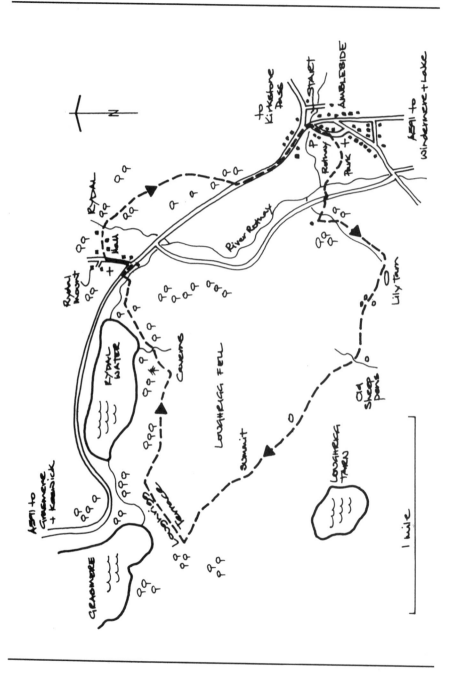

cotton grass, gradually loosing height on entering a shallow valley. Pass two ruined sheep folds to your left and bear right as you come to a wall, curving round with this. Cross the stream and follow the path which follows it upstream, gradually climbing away from the water.

Cut straight across the main path which is scarred across the plateau here, pass to the left of the small pool and walk up the path through the bracken towards the crags ahead. You'll reach a large, rather flat cairn at the far side of an area of close cropped grass. Scramble up the steep slope beyond to the little crag and then follow the path, marked by cairns, aiming for a large cairn topping a further crag some distance ahead. Just before reaching this you'll pass by a virtually dried out tarn, Black Mire, on your right.

From this, Ivy Crag, you get the best view of Loughrigg Tarn far below to your left; beyond this Elter Water and the Langdale Valleys. Sight the broad, green path which sweeps away from you and up the valley between the two highest points on Loughrigg, ahead. Walk up this path, marked by a regular line of cairns. At the point where the path splits, bear left and follow the line of cairns up the gully to reach the triangulation point on top of Loughrigg, a shade over 1100 feet above sea level. The views from this little fell are immense, taking in most of the main peaks of the Lake District. From the trig. point take a bearing along the path which strikes north-westwards and appears to tumble off the edge of Loughrigg into the left side of Grasmere. Work down from the summit to join this path.

The steep descent from the summit is made partially down an artificial, stepped path which can be treacherous in heavy rain. Eventually the path brings you to a wooded corner and a cross-path. Turn sharp right along this, known as Loughrigg Terrace, and remain with it for something over a quarter of a mile. The view across Grasmere to the village of the same name, and to the sharp ridge of Helm Crag, beyond, is exceptional. This is a well used path high above the river Rothay, evidenced by a number of bench seats provided for the more leisurely visitor.

Take the first obvious fork to the right, a point about 100 yards before the main path is joined by one from the left which comes up alongside a wall. On your new path you'll initially regain height lost on the gradual descent of the Terrace and then go slightly downhill, eventually ending up walking along the top side of a small wood. A short distance beyond this wood a path comes up from the left to join the path you are on, a point marked by a bench. Bear half right here and walk up over the little shoulder of hill to reach an area of old quarry workings. Walk across these to reach the mouth of a huge cavern, hollowed out of the hillside by slate miners over a very long period.

Take time to walk into the cavern, which contains a small lake teeming with minnows. I read in several source books that the whole population of Ambleside could easily fit inside, and that once a year a local school gives a concert in the cavern to take full benefit of the good natural acoustics. I've no reason to disbelieve either claim, but it is certain that participants in such would end up wet as there is a constant shower of water droplets cascading from the roof high above.

This huge old quarry cavern cut into Loughrigg Fell contains its own small lake.

From virtually outside this cavern a path descends in a series of bends beneath the tall pine trees. To the right of this path are further caverns created by those burrowing miners of centuries past. Carry on round with the main path, cross the stream and fall away to your left, walking down along the edge of the woods close in to your left. As the path becomes more or less level Rydal Water appears to your left, overshadowed by the bulk of Nab Scar. Fifty or so yards before you reach the woods ahead bear left to gain the lower path above the lakeside and walk along this to the kissing gate giving access to Rydal Woods.

The obvious path winds through the woods, leaving the trees at a spot above a lily-covered bay. Walk up to and cross the wooden footbridge across the Rothay and join the main road beyond. Turn right, then in about a hundred yards turn left up along the road signposted to Rydal Mount. Tiny St. Mary's Church, on your left, was Wordsworth's place of worship until his death in 1850. The meadow beyond the squat tower is Dora's Field, named by the poet after his daughter. He lived for nearly forty years in Rydal Mount, a barley-coloured house towards the top of the road you're on. His great, great, grand-daughter lives there now; a very popular place of pilgrimage for afficionados of the poet (closed Tuesdays in winter).

The route of the walk is to the right before this house is reached, it goes along the track that runs behind the driveway to Rydal Hall, signposted to a camp-site and youth centre. The large Georgian Hall is a Diocesan Retreat for the Diocese of Carlisle. It was once one of the many homes of the rich le Fleming family, from whom Wordsworth rented Rydal Mount. Wind along the rough road behind the Hall, cross the beck and walk down to the right between the cottages. Follow the footpath sign for Ambleside and join the old carriage road which sweeps across the midst of Rydal Park, after a mile or so reaching the old gate-house. Turn left along the main road to return to Ambleside a further half mile away.

13. Cunsey

Route: Bowness – Ferry – Far Sawrey – Cunsey Wood – Rawlinson Nab

Distance: 7 miles

Map: O.S. Outdoor Leisure Sheet 7, The English Lakes S.E.

Start: The Hole i' th' Wall, Bowness-on-Windermere. Grid Reference: SD 403970.

Access: Bowness is about half way down the eastern shore of Windermere and well signposted. On-street parking can be nigh on impossible during the summer; there are large, well signposted car parks at the lakeside immediately south west of the town centre. The Hole i' th' Wall is on Robinson Place, just behind St. Martin's Church in the town centre.

The Hole i' th' Wall (05394 43488)

Self proclaimed as the oldest pub in Bowness (dated 1612), the Hole' (real name The New Hall Inn) is based around one of the town's old smithies, the eponymous hole said to be that through which ale and porter were passed to the Smith and his staff when the two businesses coexisted on the same site. It can still be as hot as a furnace on a fine summers day when the patio is a proverbial sun trap and the roomy interior crowded with visitors seeking solace and escape from the hoardes in the town centre in the form of Hartleys XB, Mild and Robinsons Best Bitter. Winter is undoubtedly the best time to drink at the Hole i' th' Wall, you'll miss the explosions of colour tumbling from the hanging baskets and window boxes, but you'll also miss some of the crowds.

The main reminder that a smithy once operated here is the Old Smithy Bar, a slab-floored side room off the main area with its own small bar, games and machines, and an old plough share suspended from the roof. Here and there are occasional bellows and old farming tools once made and serviced by the cottage industry the trade represents. For the most part, however, the pub's decor and fittings vary from the esoteric to the obscure, the unmissable to the unexplainable. Take the ubiquitous stuffed animals for example; the odd rabbit, owl and bird of prey – no surprises there. Add the wolf's head and (so near as I can guess) the highland cow's head, however, and the eccentricity of the collection becomes more apparent. One part of the ceiling is hidden above a large collection of chamber pots whilst, by contrast, another section displays intricately worked wood and plaster reminiscent of grand Tudor houses.

One wall is something of a shrine to a Thomas Longmire, landlord between 1852 and 1860 and one of the most successful wrestlers of his day. For the most part the other walls are colourwashed and hung with a few prints or ornaments, leaving the massive beams, the long, hop-vine bedecked bar and the enormous old fireplace to take the eye. Charles Dickens is known to have enjoyed a few jars here in the 1850's; some of the old tables, chairs and wall benches probably date from his day, but not, I think, the highland cow.

Bowness-on-Windermere

A town which is almost entirely a product of the tourism industry, Bowness tumbles down from Windermere to the north and the craggy limestone commons in the east to the lake. There is a web of narrow streets and ginnels huddled around the old St. Martin's Church (including Robinson Place, home to the Hole i' th' Wall) but for the most part the substantial terraces of slate built houses, the grand villas and the hotels were built either for wealthy Victorian industrialists as "holiday homes" or specifically to cater for the trade that the arrival of the railway in Windermere in 1848 soon created.

Although the old town is literally a step away from the Square it is possible to escape at least some of the droves who ply their way up and down Lake Road between the restaurants, ice cream and souvenir shops and the frantic lakeside hire boat and steamer jetties. The church dates from before 1500 and is on the site of a much older place of worship, its treasures include some very early stained glass. Gravestones and memorials include some to travellers who have drowned in past accidents on the Windermere Ferry.

The few streets of three and four-storey houses and cottages behind and below the church essentially show the size of the village that existed until the Victorian explosion. Former occupations in the village include Char Fishers, the Char being a rare member of the salmon family found only in Windermere and a handful of other lakes in Britain. It was the caviar of its day and Windermere Potted was the Beluga of the Char. Bowness was also the main port on the lake. Before the turnpikes, then the railway, were built the quickest way to transport goods to and from the coastal port at Greenodd was by boat to Lakeside, at the foot of Windermere. Bowness offered a suitable pre-existing point of transfer – it was already the terminal of the cross-lake ferry, dating from medieval times – and thus gained a livelihood for a considerable number of the locals, serving the needs of the trains of pack horses and the coaches that were associated with the lakebound trade; The Stags Head Hotel, for example, is an old coaching inn.

The Walk

(This walk includes one very steep climb, gaining nearly 500 feet in as many yards).

No visit to the Lake District would be complete without a boat trip of some sort, this walk includes a return trip on the oldest of the region's lake crossings, the Windermere Ferry. Turn left out of the pub and work your way along Robinson Place, past the church and down Lake Road to the lakeside. Whilst this is the area where the tour boats are based, the ferry is some distance further south, so walk to the Tourist Information Centre and go down the road a few yards to the left of this, Rectory Road. Continue right along to its end past the cemetery, go straight across the minor road there and then follow the footpath across the fields, signposted just a couple of yards to the left of the drive which actually leads to the rectory.

Remain with this path, pass through several kissing gates and walk straight ahead across the top end of the launching area you come to on your right. A few yards beyond turn right along Ferry Nab Road and walk the remaining 200 yards to the ferry. It runs every twenty minutes from early morning to late evening every day except Christmas Day and

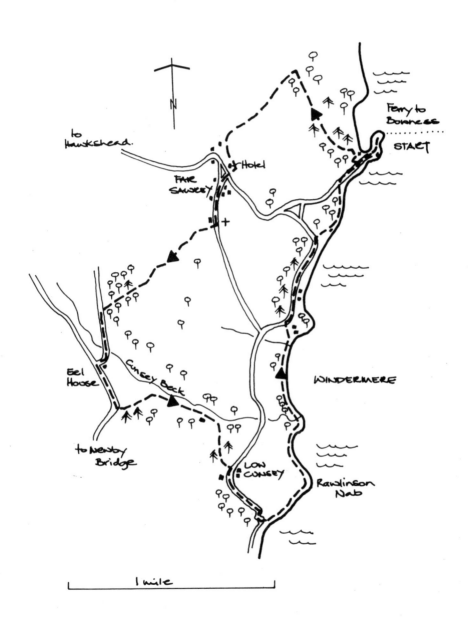

Boxing Day (and restricted on New Years Day), the pedestrian fare is (in 1991) 20 pence single. The crossing only takes about five minutes, achieved by the boat hauling itself along a cable laid across the lake bed. At the far side walk along the road. passing by the Institute of Freshwater Ecology, a leading research centre. Bend left with the road at the sign for Hawkshead and Coniston and walk along to the sharp right hand bend. Just around this is a gap in the wall on your right. Pass through this and follow the path up into the trees. In fifty or so yards turn right along the path marked by a low wall and start the steep climb up this western side of the lake shore.

The ruined building you reach is called The Station, one of the National Trust's less-renovated properties. Find the path at the far side of this (go through the left hand arch and then up beside the large fallen tree) and continue the steep climb, the route marked here and there by white spots painted on trees or posts. It's a very pleasant woodland walk through mature oak, yew, beech and sycamore and well used as one access to a very popular walk along the length of Claife Heights, the low fells you're now walking. Virtually at the top of the climb turn right at the sign for Hawkshead and walk along the ridge, a fence to your left. Frequent gaps through the trees allow glimpses down to the lake and across to Bowness, Windermere and the fells around the Kentmere Horseshoe and the bottom end of High Street.

Half a mile's pleasant stroll brings you to a kissing gate and an old cart track. Once through the gate turn left along this track, signposted for Hawkshead and Sawrey. Wind along with this walled track, passing through gates as appropriate and favouring the track for Far Sawrey at the split. There are glorious views from this modest height across the expanse of Grizedale Forest to the south and, to the right (west), over to the mountains around Coniston. Remain with the track and wind down to the main road at Far Sawrey. Turn right along this. Those who've already worked up a thirst can quench it here at the Sawrey Hotel (open all day, Theakstons) or at the adjoining old stables, now converted into the Claife Crier Bar (Theakstons, Jennings, closed from 3pm-6pm). This is named after a boggart (ghost) which was said to once haunt the wooded hills behind the hotel, crying out for the ferry to cross the lake during foggy weather in the hope that it would flounder.

Take the narrow road opposite the hotel's beer garden, signposted for the church, and wind down past the few old farms and cottages that are Far Sawrey. Walk past the cottages at Town End, the church off to your left, and look on your right, immediately past white-painted Rose and Dove cottages, for a public footpath sign. Go through the kissing gate and then follow the path ahead which cuts a terrace around the hillside on the right of the field ten yards or so into the field. Pass through a few gates and climb a stile, keeping the main stand of woods off to your right on Castle Hill. Climb the stile at the end of the last pasture and then follow the obvious path through the oak and birch woodland for about half a mile, keeping the fence close to your left throughout.

On reaching the minor road turn left, pausing only to appreciate the unusual road sign to your right. Keeping half an eye out for the supposed beneficiaries of this salutary warning (dewey summer mornings or evenings are best), simply walk along to the T-junction at Eel House and turn left along this wider road. After about a quarter of a mile, at the point where the road bends right and starts a steep uphill climb, a public footpath sign directs you left for Cunsey Bridge. Follow this somewhat muddy path alongside the recently felled and replanted woodland, a part of the huge Graythwaite Estate. Simply remain with this path, eventually entering the woodlands proper. Off to the left the torrents of Cunsey Beck echo through the trees, the path here and there bordered by great swathes of irises and rushes. The old barn shortly passed by on your right is named on maps as The Forge, certainly the evidence of the heavily coppiced hazels in the woods suggests that the raw material for charcoal was once cut in the area, charcoal for centuries being used to fuel a forge.

Shortly after passing this, bear right with the wide track as it rounds the corner of a wall and walk ahead into the fir woods, bearing left at the junction a few yards further on. Remain with this forest road through the rather gloomy woods to emerge on a minor road opposite Low Cunsey Farm and turn right along this. Stay with this quiet back road for about half a mile, passing by an estate lodge house on your right.

Wind round the sharp bends and just as you reach a stone barn on your left look for the footpath sign also on your left. Climb the stile here and walk along the narrow path to gain the lake shore. For the next mile-and-a-half stick with this lakeside path, darting in and out of the trees and rounding the pretty little promontory known as Rawlinson Nab.

The path takes you across two footbridges – in summer look for thousands of minnows in the first beck, Cunsey Beck – and alongside a wildlife refuge (in fact most of the shoreline seems to be a refuge). Walk as far as you can get and then veer away from the shoreline immediately this side of a renovated boat-house, shortly reaching a minor road. Turn right and follow this for nearly a mile to reach a lane dropping steeply off to your right and signposted Bryers Cottage. It's also signposted as private, but a permissive path has been established so walk down the drive, past the cottage and back to the lakeshore, remaining with this for a further quarter of a mile. On your left here the Cumbria Naturalists Trust have established Ash Landing Nature Reserve, open for occasional visits during the summer (see notices posted locally).

Once you regain the main road walk ahead along it to return to the ferry and, having recrossed Windermere, retrace your original route back into the centre of Bowness (you can if you wish bear left soon after crossing the top end of the launching site and walk around the lakeside Cockshott Point (National Trust) to return to Bowness).

14. Underbarrow

Route: Underbarrow – Cunswick Scar – Scout Scar – Barrowfield

Distance: 7 Miles

Map: O.S. Outdoor Leisure Series Sheet 7, The English Lakes, SE.

Start: The Underbarrow Punch Bowl. Grid Reference: SD 468922

Access: The scattered village of Underbarrow is about three miles west of Kendal on the minor road between there and Crosthwaite. The pub is the first building you come to on your left (not to be confused with The Punchbowl in nearby Crosthwaite).

The Underbarrow Punchbowl (04488 234)

In this low, whitewashed old pub I quaffed easily the best pint of Bass I can remember quaffing outside of the fabled Coopers Tavern in Burton on Trent (the brewery tap). Add to this the setting, in craggy, limestone country perched above the lush valley of the River Lyth and you've got a corner of old Westmorland well worth seeking out.

The pub is of indeterminate age. You don't, however, find many priest holes constructed after about 1660, so the unusual example of such, now exposed behind the small bar, gives the Punchbowl a good 300 years service to the community. Much of this service was dedicated to persons employed in the woollen trade. Nearby Kendal was one of England's major woollen towns, exporting much of this product through the docks at Ulverston. The hilly route between these two towns was served at regular intervals by wayside taverns where pack and cart horses could be changed over and waggoners eat and sleep. The Underbarrow Punchbowl was one such tavern; earlier this century a smithy and smiths cottage stood at the far end of what is now the pub car park, fittings related to the shaping of old wheel rims remain set into enormous blocks below the pub's wayside sign.

One person to witness such activity would have been William Pearson who lived in the village until early this century. He was reputed to have been the last survivor of the famous "Charge of the Light Brigade" during the Crimean War in 1854. And yes, he did claim to have been treated by Florence Nightingale. He saw out his twilight years as a Fellmongerer (similar to a tanner) in this quiet corner of Lakeland.

The Punchbowl, Underbarrow: the priest-hole behind the bar bears evidence of the pub's 300 years of service to the community

The pub is popular with walkers, being on the Westmorland Way (an offshoot of the Coast to Coast Walk) and acts as a regular meeting spot for rambling clubs from many points of the compass. The one small bar serves two low beamed rooms reservedly decorated with old pewter tankards, copper oddments and horse brasses. The larger of the rooms hosts an enormous old fireplace, dated back to around 1700; a spice cupboard fitted into the wall next to it – presumably to help keep the spices dry – is dated 1739.

A range of bar meals is available seven days a week; the pub is open from 11am to 3pm (4pm Saturdays) and 6-11pm. Landlord Mr Howarth may extend these hours during the summer months. Children are welcomed and larger parties can be catered for, by prior arrangement, in a function room.

The Walk

On leaving the pub turn right and walk up the road for about 200 yards to reach, on your left, the driveway to Tranthwaite Hall. This is also a public footpath so turn along it and remain with it for about a quarter of a mile. Immediately before reaching a cottage on your left look on your right to find a public footpath sign, somewhat overgrown, beside a kissing gate. Pass through this gate and walk up the pasture, passing by two waymarkers attached to pylons. The next waymark is on a short post, from here bear off to the right and walk up to the small knoll capped by oak trees. From here walk across the rough pasture to the kissing gate you'll see at the butt-end of the wall ahead (where it joins the wall to the left at right angles). Once through this gate take a bearing on the transmitter mast on the escarpment top ahead and walk towards this.

Already, to your left, distant views to the peaks around the Kentmere Horseshoe have opened out whilst a glance behind reveals extensive views across the southern mountains of the Lakes. A line of waymarked posts will bring you to a corner of the pasture. Cross the surfaced farm driveway here and pass through the gate giving access to the high-hedged bridleway known as Gamblesmire Lane. In spring and summer this overflows with a profusion of foxgloves and dog roses, celendine and woodspurge. Continue with the track up through the pleasant, shady area of broadleaf woodland, go through the difficult to open gate at the top (you need to lift it a good 6 inches before the catch will work) and continue on up the field keeping the wall to your right. Just before reaching the top corner look to the left along the top wall to find a kissing gate; pass through this and turn left, then walking along the line of the wall.

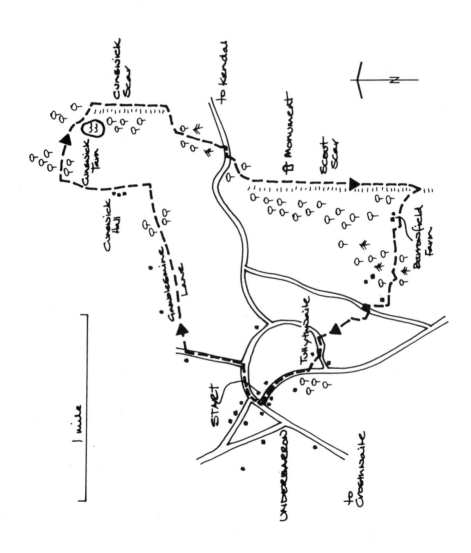

Most walkers tackle the limestone scars this walk is aiming for from the Kendal side. The views you'll be enjoying from this section of the walk, however, amply emphasise the advantage of tackling the walk from this west side. To your left (west) the horizon is a mass of jumbled peaks; The Langdale Pikes and Great Gable are easily recognisable, less familiar ones include the Crinkle Crags and the group based around The Old Man of Coniston.

Opposite Cunswick Hall farm pass through the kissing gate, walk across the field road and join the wall on your left for about twenty yards, then go through a further kissing gate and turn right along the surfaced roadway. Cross the cattle grid and then leave the roadway to curve away to the left, instead remaining with the wall to your right. Walk on past the first small area of woodland and on to the second. About twenty yards beyond the start of this second wood keep your eyes peeled for a narrow gap stile. Go through this and follow the obvious path through this corner of the woods, carpeted with wood anemones and ramson. Leave the woods at the next gap stile, turn left and look to the far right hand corner of the field to spot a gate in the corner, then walking across to this.

Pass through this gate (the small gate, not the field gate), pausing to appreciate Cunswick Tarn, nestling beneath the limestone scar that shares it's name. Walk along the narrow path between the woods and the thistle-rich tarn end and, having climbed the stile, bear left and follow the steepening main path up through the woodland to emerge at the top of the scar a short while later. Go through the kissing gate here and turn right, walking along the obvious path alongside the fence/wall that parallels the edge of Cunswick Scar. In summer you won't see anything of the Tarn far below, although in winter and early spring the leafless trees should afford a glimpse.

Remain with the line of the wall and woodland edge as the track veers away to the left and, at the end, bear right around the corner of the wall to a four-fingered footpath post. Follow the direction indicated as a concessionary path to Scout Scar and keep the wall to your right. A second sign directs you into woodland, once within which just keep right at any splits in the path. You'll soon pass by the small transmitter and, within yards, come to a small car park in an old quarry. Turn right down along the minor road for a few yards and then go through the kissing gate on the left, once through which bear right and walk up the well used path to gain the summit level of Scout Scar. A stroll of a few hundred yards will get you to the viewpoint near the summit.

This vista of the Central Mountains and the countryside below Cunswick Scar is the reward for those who persevere to the summit.

A cupola-type affair crowns this point. Look around the inner rim of this curious structure to discover its *raison d'être* – it's a kind of toposcope. Painted around this inside rim is a rough representation of the shape of the horizon throughout the 360 degree sweep of this viewpoint, with all the main peaks – including Scafell Pike, England's highest at 3210 feet – named. On the clearest of days it is said you can see two other altitudinous "S's", Snowdon in North Wales and Snaefel on the Isle of Man.

Leave the cupola and continue to walk south along the Scar's edge. Down below the thick woodlands are patrolled by jay and magpie, jackdaws nest on the cliffs and buzzard pick up useful thermals to glide high before quartering their territory. When you reach a point high above Barrowfield Farm (down to your right) start to look for the path that hairpins to the right and descends steeply down the face of the Scar – it's just below a large cairn. Walk on through the woods and join the track that leads to the farm. Follow the waymarkers round the back of the farmyard, go through the gate and walk to the signpost beneath the holly tree. Turn right here towards Garth Row Lane, walk past the farmhouse and turn left at the next signpost, walking down the field to the woods. Climb the stone step stile here and then follow the, initially steep, path through the woods; the path is well waymarked.

Walk virtually straight over the pasture you encounter and re-enter the woods at the stone step stile (about 25 yards to the left of the power cables). Once again follow the waymarkers down through the woods, here largely conifers; keep an eye out for red squirrels which are common hereabouts or a brightly coloured crossbill feeding on pine-cone seeds. Leave the woods and head across the pasture, aiming to the right of the low knoll and walking towards the lone Scots pine at the far side. Turn right with the wall here and walk along the path beside the cottage, then along the driveway to the minor road. Turn left along this road and in a matter of yards go through the gate on the right at the public footpath sign.

Walk along the track for a few yards to the point where the wall bends left. Here, bear half right and head for the far corner of the field, a tall hedge on your left. Go over the stile at this corner and head diagonally left across the next pasture, aiming for the short stretch of stone wall in the far boundary. Climb the step stile here, cross the brook and then head slightly right, aiming for the pylon you can see just behind the oak tree. Look for the stile giving access to the minor road and turn left along this. Wind along with it past Tullythwaite Garth House and then look for the footpath sign, on the left but pointing right along an old driveway beneath an enormous plane tree. Go along this drive to the old garage. Turn left in front of the garage, don't go into the field beside it but do plunge down through the heavily overgrown old garden/ pasture, keeping an old wall to your right and roughly following the line of pylons. On reaching the minor road turn right and remain with this for the remaining half mile back to Underbarrow. Turn right at the T-junction to return to the pub.

15. Sizergh

Route: Sizergh – Levens Bridge – Sedgwick – Larkrigg

Distance: 4.5 Miles

Map: O.S. Pathfinder sheet 627, Milnthorpe.

Start: The Strickland Arms, Sizergh. Grid Reference: SD 500873.

Access: Sizergh is a scatter of farms, hotels and houses virtually beneath the major junction of the A6, A590 and A591 roads about 4 miles south west of Kendal. Follow the brown road signs for Sizergh Castle, the pub is a few yards from the driveway leading to this.

The Strickland Arms (05395 60239)

Sizergh Castle, now a National Trust property, is the ancestral home of the Stricklands, an influential local family who can include the powerful Bishop Strickland, once Bishop of Carlisle, in their family tree. No prizes, then, for guessing where the pub picked up its name.

The solid, three storey stone road-house lives largely on the excellent reputation it's bar meals and Theakston's Best Bitter and XB have amongst both locals and visitors. It's also busy with passing trade from visitors to the Castle and to the riverside caravan park a short distance away. For all its grandiose architecture – huge ornate chimneys, stone-mullioned windows and large dormer portals – the pub is surprisingly compact internally. The one bar serves a large room well, almost plushly, appointed with thick carpet, mocquette seats and a selection of old benches and pews. The pool table and slot machine are tucked away in virtually a side room off the main public area.

Outside is a steep beer garden dotted with tables and benches, although it can suffer from the noise of traffic on the busy A591 at weekends and in summer.

Opening hours vary during the year but bar meals are generally available from noon to 2pm and 7 to 10pm – look for the ever-changing specials detailed on the blackboard beside the bar.

Sizergh Castle

In common with many large, medieval houses in the north of England, Sizergh is based on an old Pele Tower, a solid, foursquare lump of masonry with walls several feet thick built as a place of refuge from those maurauding Scots of yore and into which would decant the local population, complete with livestock, when trouble threatened. Over the centuries additional wings and floors were added to produce the polymorphous building evident today. Strangely, having been built as a defence against Scots, many of the prized exhibits in the castle celebrate later Scottish ventures, the Jacobite Rebellions for example. The Castle is justly renowned for its gardens and grounds, including vast rock gardens and a lake, part of an old moat. The Castle and Estate are managed by the National Trust and are open from April to October (inclusive) each afternoon except Fridays and Saturdays.

The Walk

With your back to the Strickland Arms turn right and walk along the minor road to the busy A590 dual carriageway. In summer the verges of this back road are smothered with the bright blue flowers of Meadow Crane's Bill. Turn right and walk along the pavement beside the main road, in about 200 yards crossing to the other side to walk beside the lodge and down the narrow Force Lane. Immediately before the group of cottages towards the end of this lane, just as it starts to descend, look on the right for a public footpath sign to Levens Bridge. Go over the stone step stile here and follow the obvious track across the field, shortly joining a band of woodland on your left. These woods are a deer sanctuary, a part of the estate of Levens Hall.

In a couple of hundred yards climb over the solid stone stile on the left to gain access to this parkland. The public footpath through this, the sole

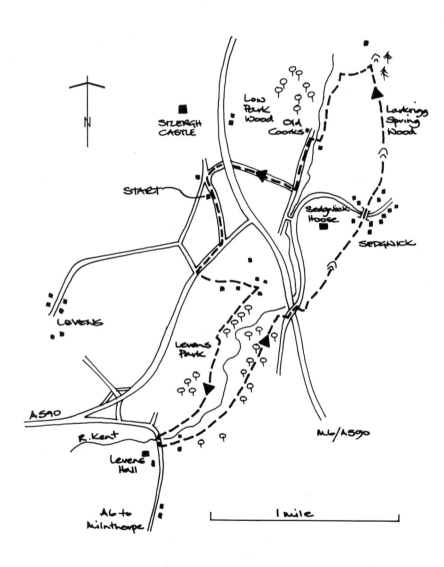

N

SIZERGH
CASTLE

Low
Park
Wood

Old
Cooks

Larkrigg
Spring
Wood

START

Sedgwick
House

SEDGWICK

LEVENS

Levens
Park

A590

R. Kent

M6/A590

Levens
Hall

A6 to
Milnthorpe

1 mile

survivor of over a dozen deer parks around Kendal, is well waymarked and gradually falls away down the hillside towards the River Kent. The parkland is grazed by two unusual breeds of herbivore, black fallow deer and Bagot Goats. The deer are, indeed, virtually black on their backs and head with very dark grey-brown underbelly and legs. The Bagot Goats, named after the family who built (and remain domiciled at) Levens Hall, have a passing resemblance to Soay Sheep. Their origins, however, are somewhat more distant, having been brought back by Richard the First from a Crusade and presented to the family when the Monarch stayed at Levens Hall. Both deer and sheep are relatively tame and you're almost sure to see plenty of both at close quarters.

In a little over half a mile you'll get to a gate which disgorges you onto the north end of Levens Bridge. Cross the bridge (but not the road) to find a similar gate taking you back into the Park and a footpath which gradually climbs up and away from the River Kent. Should you wish to visit Levens Hall, then cross both the bridge and the road.

Levens Hall

The Hall needs little introduction as the location of one of Europe's greatest topiary gardens, geometric and "flight of fancy" shapes being teased into shape over several centuries from box and yew trees. Many of the original designs were the work of Guillaume Beaumont, one-time gardener By Appointment to King James the Second. As with Sizergh, the house is based around a Pele Tower, but its real glory lies in the surviving Elizabethan stonework, carvings and furniture, supported by a Pandora's Box of artefacts once owned by such luminaries as Nelson and Napoleon. The Hall is also home to a large collection of both model and full size steam engines, cars and wagons, regularly worked during the summer. The Hall is open throughout the summer from 11am to 5pm.

For a good half-mile or so the footpath follows one of the most spectacular avenue of oaks in England, planted in parkland laid out by Monsieur Beaumont nearly three centuries ago when Good Queen Anne was on the throne. Through the trees you'll get occasional glimpses of the Howgill and Shap Fells to the east and north of Kendal.

At the end of the avenue of trees climb the stile beside the gate to your right and walk the few yards up to the minor road. Turn left along this and cross the bridge over the A591. Immediately beyond this, on the right, is a service road; immediately beyond this a path climbs the bank to a half hidden public footpath sign to Hawes Bridge. Climb the stile here and turn left along the line of the fence for about twenty yards, then angle right roughly along the line of the electricity pylons. Look ahead across the field to find an arched bridge, an incongruous stone structure in the middle of the field, and walk to this.

This bridge is an old overbridge across the former Lancaster Canal. From this side there is no evidence (other than the bridge..) that such a waterway existed; on the other side, however, you can discern the general outline of the canal and the tow-path. Go through the kissing gate beneath the bridge and walk along the narrow path which follows the old tow-path. Off to the left the Gothic edifice of Sedgwick Hall draws the eye. It was built in this style in mid-Victorian times by William Wakefield, a rich local industrialist. It is now converted, inevitably, into luxury apartments (funny, isn't it, why every conversion of any old building always produces luxury...?).

Bridges, like this one at Larkrigg, span the former Lancaster Canal.

The walk follows the old canal for the next mile and more. In a short distance a graceful aqueduct and embankment takes the canal above the village of Sedgwick, to which there is access if required down a flight of steps from the northern end of the aqueduct. Beyond this structure the canal has been converted into a sunken garden. Once past this the path debouches into an open field where, again, the only evidence of the old canal is another ivy covered old bridge. At the far end of the field the canal again becomes apparent as it enters a stretch of woodland, Larkrigg Spring, a very pleasant section of the walk with shafts of sunlight dappling the old canal trough, here copiously filled with wildflowers, willow, damson and wayfarer trees.

The far end of the wood reveals the best preserved section of the canal, the tow-path clearly delineating the west bank, an old winding hole (where boats could be turned) still easily discernible and the wide, stone lined trough disappearing beneath another bridge. The canal was surveyed by the renowned engineer John Rennie and opened in 1819, linking Preston with Kendal via Lancaster. It was a "broad" canal, that is the locks were 14 feet wide rather than the more usual 7 feet, and meant that barges carrying up to fifty tons could reach Kendal. The main cargoes were limestone and coal. Passengers were also catered for; an express service was introduced in 1835 taking eight hours to travel between Preston and Kendal and a phenomenal three hours on the lock-free stretch between Preston and Lancaster – about 10mph!

Unfortunately, the fact that this northern stretch of the canal was built over limestone meant that there were continual problems with water loss, and breaches were fairly common. The last regular traffic was coal for Kendal Power Station which continued until 1944 when the LMS Railway, by then owners of the canal, officially abandoned it through a "broadbrush" Act of Parliament that also saw many other canals throughout Britain abandoned. The northern section beyond Carnforth was quickly drained in many sections and infilled. In 1968 the M6 cut across the line at field level just to the north of Tewitfield Locks, about nine miles south of Kendal, effectively ruling out any chance of reopening this stretch of the waterway, despite strong local support.

Immediately before reaching this next overbridge there is a small gap-stile in the wall on your left. Go through this and follow the well used path across to the far left corner of the field where a gate gives access to a wide track. Walk along this and swing left with it to join a wide track above this eastern bank of the Kent. You'll get glimpses of the river through the trees, the far bank and islands are infested with giant hogweed and butterbur. Cross the delicate wood and metal suspension footbridge and walk ahead to the narrow road.

In the woodlands to the right here, an area now given over to a caravan park, can be seen the remains of a large gunpowder mill. This commodity became increasingly important in the Eighteenth and Nineteenth centuries as the amount of quarrying in Westmorland expanded to meet the growing markets created by the industrial revolution. The River Kent in this area was harnessed to provide water power for grinding and mixing the necessary ingredients and a number of works were opened up by the Wakefield family (of Sedgwick Hall). Charcoal was a major ingredient and the locally profligate Alder Buckthorn tree was a particularly favoured raw material for this.

Turn left along this minor road and walk on to the junction about a quarter of a mile away. Turn right here, the Strickland Arms being signposted along with Sizergh and Levens. Cross under the road bridge a further third of a mile on and bear left at the end to find the pub.

16. Burton - in - Kendal

Route: Burton-in-Kendal – Uberash – Hutton Roof – Crag House

Distance: 7 miles

Map: O.S. Pathfinder Sheet 637, Burton-in-Kendal and Caton.

Start: The King's Arms, Burton-in-Kendal. Grid Reference: SD 531765

Access: Burton-in-Kendal is about 4 miles north east of Carnforth on the A6070, the old road between Lancaster and Kendal. The King's Arms is about half way along the village street on the left, you can hardly miss the enormous pub sign. Park, with permission, in the pub car park, on-street parking is very restricted.

The King's Arms (0524 781409)

This solid, three storey stone and pebble-dashed building stands a few yards from the village square, or, at least, the site of the market cross at a point where the one main street widens out. Inside, the pub is remarkably compact with one bar serving several distinct drinking areas. The bar is straight in front of you as you enter, built of mellow wood and with leaded glass panels in the cornices. The main room is to the right, warmed by an open log fire, carpeted and comfortably, if not opulently, furnished. The walls are adorned with a restrained collection of old photographs, posters, walking sticks and foxes brushes and masks; a patient taxidermist took the trouble to stuff a weasel and this is hidden in one corner. An adjoining room, approached through an arch, is largely set aside for diners and there is a separate games room. Mitchell's Best Bitter and Mild are on offer, with the stronger ESB as an occasional guest.

The King's Arms is an old coaching inn and the back courtyard still has the old cobbles, chipped and marked by countless coaches. The substantial outbuildings will have once acted as stables and, undoubtedly, as a brewhouse. The pub was an important meeting place for merchants; Burton was once one of the premier corn markets of England

and the wealth generated by this trade is reflected in the fine yeoman's houses and merchant's mansions that vie with overhanging cottages and barns to front the main street, behind which a web of ginnels (passageways) run between cart-roads and village pastures and haymeadows.

The Walk

Leave the tiny square in the village centre and walk up the path to the left of the Post Office, climbing steadily between thick hedges towards the lone Scots Pine. Bear left below this tree, following the obvious path along the line of wall at the top of the fields, passing through a series of kissing gates to reach a minor road. Views to the left across to the mountains of the southern Lakes are, even from this altitude, already extensive.

Cross straight over the minor road and join the walled/hedged track opposite, signposted as a bridleway to Burton Fell and evidently well used as such. For the next mile or so this path gradually gains height, weaving in and out of woodland and skirting the Cumbria Wildlife Trust's Lancelot Clark Storth Nature Reserve, protecting this lower edge of the outcropping limestone which hosts a profusion of wild orchids, celendine, bluebell and dog mercury. Keep left at the fork and follow the line of the wall to your left, soon passing through the gap in this to walk along through to the edge of the woods. Go through the gate here and walk ahead across the pastures to the minor road.

Turn right and walk up the modest but continuous gradient to the top. A glance behind reveals an ever expanding view across this corner of Cumbria to an unsurpassed panorama of the southern Lake's mountains – Harter Fell, Ill Bell, Coniston Old Man and the Langdale Pikes for example. Further south the broken coastline of Furness and Cartmel and the sweep of Morecambe Bay offer a contrast. On reaching the footpath sign on your right and delineating the Limestone Link Footpath to Hutton Roof, enter the rough pasture and follow the obvious path south east.

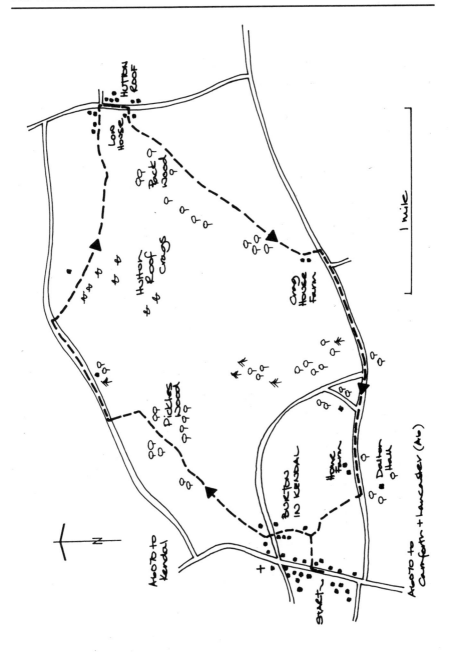

This path sticks closely to the edge of a large plateau of limestone pavement on your right known as Uberash, or Hutton Roof Crags, an area rich in juniper, broom, gorse and scrubby ash woodland and with many lime loving plants. To the left are immense views over the Vale of Lune to the high Pennines, to the Fells above Appleby and Brough, the distinct peak of Ingleborough and Leck Fell, the highest point in Lancashire. Behind you the massif of the Howgills forms the horizon.

Essentially just follow the obvious path roughly along the edge of the Pavement and you'll eventually start to gently descend, at which point an outcropping ridge of limestone strikes across in front of you. Bear left here with the path and walk along the foot of this ridge, a favourite spot for climbers, then angle up to the lowest point in the ridge, marked by a stunted, gnarled Phillyrea tree. Ahead of you now are several more ridges of limestone to work your way through. The path through the bracken and small thorn bushes is obvious and soon the hamlet of Hutton Roof becomes visible, laid out like a model village in the vale far below. Simply follow the wide path down through the bracken and occasional crag of limestone. Off to your right near the bottom is a pedestal rock, formed by the action of rain and groundwater dissolving away a basal layer of limestone leaving a large block perched on a narrow pedestal. Pass just above the enormous Sycamore and join the line of wall on your right. Bend right with this, go through the gate and walk down the rough lane to the village road.

Turn right and follow this one main street for about 300 yards to the telephone box, just beyond which is a public footpath sign, on the right, dedicated for Crag House. There's also a long, ground level drinking trough formed from the village brook at this point. Walk up through the farmyard and between the barns here at Low House Farm, go through the gate at the rear and along the subsequent track past the remains of countless old vehicles and agricultural machinery. In a short while an information board outlines the history and attractions of the Park Wood National Nature Reserve, up to your right. You need a permit to enter this, so remain with and continue along the main track.

You'll soon reach a second information board beside an offset field gate on your right. Here, go through this gate and follow the field track beyond, slowly gaining a little height to reach the top corner of this long, narrow pasture. Climb the stone step stile beyond the information board here and walk ahead, slightly favouring your right hand. Once across the stone-slab footbridge over the stream walk on ahead to the shallow valley between the low ridges of limestone. In the past this rock has been put to good use locally, the remains of a limekiln stare blankly out from the snout of the ridge on your right. The ridge on your left soon peters out but remain on line, ignoring the track as it bends right to pass through a small gap and up a higher valley. Instead, keep the ridge, then hedge/fence to your right, scrubby woodland soon appearing behind this fence. Remain outside these woods and pass through a line of stiles, always keeping the fence/woods to your immediate right, eventually gaining a rutted track leading gently down to the farmyard at Crag House. Walk through this and then down the drive to the minor road, whereupon turn right.

Remain with this quiet back-road for nearly two miles, ignoring the various turnings to left or right. Pass by Home Farm on your right (the only building you reach, with a large walled garden and stable-tower clock) and at the next bend, about 200 yards further on, go through the field gate on the right – there's the pole of an old footpath sign just to the right. Walk along the path beyond this and into the long, narrow field, continuing across this to the offset corner where there is a gap stile at the end of the short wall. From this corner head diagonally across the field to the kissing gate and, from here, aim for the lone Scots Pine beyond the next field. Pass through the gap stile your side of this tree and bear left to walk down the hedged pathway back to Burton Post Office.

Captured on canvas – looking towards the Duddon Valley and Harter Fell

Lancashire-over-the-Sands

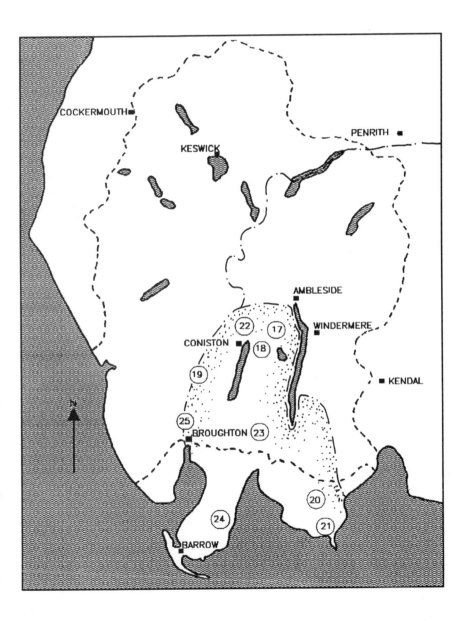

17. Hawkshead

Route: Hawkshead – Outgate – Blelham Tarn – High Wray – Latterbarrow

Distance: 6 miles

Map: O.S. Outdoor Leisure Series Sheet 7; The English Lakes, S.E.

Start: The Queen's Head, Hawkshead. Grid Reference: SD 353982.

Access: Hawkshead is easily reached from Bowness-on-Windermere via the cross lake ferry (pedestrians and vehicles) which runs every twenty minutes from early morning to late evening (check for the last return sailing from the western terminus). Hawkshead is about three miles beyond the western terminus, simply remain with the main road, the B5285, which skirts the eastern shore of Esthwaite Water. From Ambleside take the A593 towards Coniston and turn onto the B5286 in Clappersgate, about a mile south-west of Ambleside; Hawkshead is then about four miles along this road. In all cases park in the large pay-car-park to the east of the village centre.

The Queen's Head (09666 271)

Tucked away off one of Hawkshead's tiny squares beside the imaginatively-named Main Street, The Queen's Head looks, at first sight, to be something of a sham. The black-and-white exterior seems a little too symmetrical to be true, the render and stonework just that bit too regular to belong to centuries past. Once through the low entrance door, however, such reservations are quickly dispelled. Only our short cousins from the reign of Elizabeth the First would have contrived to build a pub with beams so low, whilst the magnificently wood-panelled main room oozes age and character.

These panelled walls groan under the weight of myriad paintings, prints, plaques and plates, brass bellows, serving dishes and oddities such as part of an old pump. The oddest artefact, however, is the enormous old shoe, known as the Girt Clog, mounted in a trophy case above the fireplace in the main room and looking for all the world like a taxidermist's efforts on a mis-shapen tench. The story goes that it was a one-off order made by a local cobbler for the village molecatcher (whatever happened to them – it would look great in the appropriate space in a passport..), John Waterson, which unfortunate contracted elephantitis in the 1820's and needed such footwear to fit his deformed limb. Undoubtedly a much better conversation piece than a stuffed fish. Near to the bar is an evocative collection of old photographs of the Windermere Car Ferries of yesteryear.

The pub is a great place to be on a winter's day during the festive season. The pub's very framework bows under the weight of decorations whilst the small fire in the red-bricked fireplace defies the laws of physics in the level of heat it produces: you'll all-but melt if you're based on the settles next to the fire. Warming you internally could be a gigantic bar meal, the pub prides itself on offering quality food and you'd have to travel many a mile to match such offerings, good enough even to tempt you away from the Hartley's XB and Robinson's Best Bitter currently on offer at the bar (although, as in the case of any Hartley's pub, the choice of beer in 1992 may well change as the Ulverston brewery is due to be closed). The Queen's Head is open all day every day (i.e. 11am to 11pm), standard hours on Sundays.

Hawkshead

The village's reputation precedes it. The compact old settlement is probably the most popular spot in the Lake District, and as the Lake District is one of the most visited National Parks in Europe this means Popular with a capital "P." On a summer's weekend the place is heaving, the car parks clogged and the approach roads a gladiatorial field fought over by coaches and caravans.

Midweek and/or out of high season, however, the village takes on a totally different character. This is the time to stroll around the interconnecting squares, yards and alleyways, to best appreciate the medieval, timber framed overhanging cottages with their solid, external stone staircases, galleries and extensions supported precariously on slender pillars of slate. You may miss out on some of the attractions (such as the Beatrix Potter Gallery and Wordsworth's old school) which tend to be open on a regular basis only in midsummer but the ability to move around freely (and, more importantly for any self respecting reader of this book, to get a seat inside one of the pubs) more than makes up for this.

The village grew up as an important wool market, a trade largely controlled by the Prior of Furness Abbey within whose demesne the village lay. At the height of its prosperity in the Sixteenth Century Hawkshead rivalled Ambleside and Kendal as a centre of the wool trade; it even had a market charter granted, another measure of its importance. The wool trade, however, was fickle and only Kendal retained its position in this market. Hawkshead found a new lease of life as a centre for charcoal burning, the charcoal being used to smelt the copper and iron ores gouged from the higher fells which form a distant horizon to the village. In many of the broadleaf woodlands around the village the evidence of coppicing (harvesting the trees to provide branches of an ideal thickness for creating charcoal) can still be seen.

The tiny market square once echoed to the sounds of trains of pack horses conveying not only charcoal or metalliferous ores but also salt en route from the coast to the market towns of the high Pennines; there were once seven inns catering for this trade, places where merchants could base themselves for a few days whilst transacting business. The little yards either side of The Red Lion, the oldest surviving pub, are redolent of the days when such deals were struck. Here also the pack horse trains would be corralled. The juggernauts of their day, trains of twenty or thirty animals were under the control of a jagger and his young assistant and were a common sight, particularly in the rural upland areas of Britain. The wealth generated by such business helped pay for the building and rebuilding of St. Micheal's Church which stands aloof on its own mound beside the village.

The Walk

Turn right from the Queens Head and walk for a few yards along the pedestrianised stretch of the High Street. Just before reaching the Red Lion go right, beneath the low archway and into one of the old yards behind the pub, still lined by old cottages and stables/barns. Go through

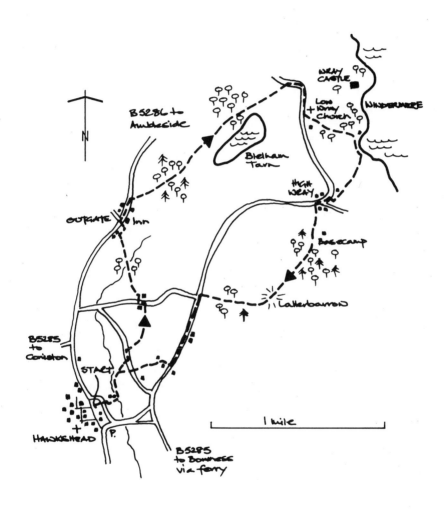

the gate at the far end and cross straight over the by-pass road, going down the lane opposite. In a few yards bear right at the footpath sign and wind around with the lane which soon deteriorates to a footpath. At the far end cross the footbridge and turn left, then after a short while angle to the right across the field, following the well trodden path.

Having passed through several kissing gates bear left at the sign for Loanthwaite. Go through a couple of stiles to reach an old Green Lane and turn left along this. In a matter of fifty or so yards take the path through the gate beneath the oak tree on your right. Stick to the line of the hedge/fence on your right, climb a stile a short distance later and continue to a further stile beside a field gate on your right. Climb this, turn left to reach a minor road and then turn left along this and walk through the area of farm buildings.

Just past the farm house look on your right for a public footpath sign for Outgate and High Wray. Go through the gate here and along the subsequent track for a few yards, looking on your left for the sign for Outgate affixed to a gatepost. Climb the stile here and then go diagonally right across the rough pasture to a ladder stile over the short stretch of remaining wall. Once over this head for the oak woods on the far side of the field, entering them on the faint path beside the upright stone slab, probably the remnant of an old gate. Towards the end of the woods go left at the fork, ford a brook and head for the stile, once over which aim for the large sycamore tree in the far corner of the field.

Just past this tree walk along the short walled pathway and turn right at the end (after the kissing gate). Walk up through the small pasture to reach another kissing gate, this one behind The Outgate Inn in the hamlet of the same name. This is another fine Hartleys establishment worthy of investigation, the landlord obviously has connections with the world of jazz and there are regular evenings of such entertainment.

Pass in front of the pub and continue northwards along the road towards Ambleside, ignoring the first signed footpath on your right. A short way beyond the last house in the village you'll find a Bridleway sign on your right, next to the roadside village nameboard. Join this bridleway and remain with it through and beside the woodland, in half a mile or so you'll see the beautiful, isolated little Blelham Tarn down to your right. It belongs to the National Trust but as it's a nature reserve waterside paths are undeveloped so remain with the path you are on, soon passing through an area of birch woodland. On reaching the minor road turn right and follow this for the next half mile or so.

Blelham Tarn, near Outgate, is a National Trust nature reserve

Just past the Gothic style gate-house turn left up the driveway to the isolated little church of St. Margarets at Low Wray. This was built in the 1850's for a rich Liverpool surgeon, James Dawson, as part of a package which includes a mock castle, now used as a nautical training school, on a wooded hillside overlooking Windermere. A past parson at the church was Hardwicke Rawnsley, one of the three founders of the National Trust at the end of the last century. The last vicar to have the living of the Parish as one separate from that of Hawkshead preached his last sermon there in 1952, an incredible 57 years after preaching his first there.

Immediately past the driveway leading to the church a Bridleway is signposted, left, which brings you gently down to the western shore of Windermere. Turn right and walk south for a short distance, the lake to your left. On the far side of the water you can see the Lake District Visitors Centre at Brockhole and behind this the distinct peak of Wansfell. Go through the gate behind the boat-house and then turn right at the footpath signposted for High Wray. Simply keep to the right of the pastures and you'll eventually climb a stone step stile which leads onto a gravelled lane. Turn right, walk to the minor road and then turn left and walk up past the scattering of cottages and farms which is High Wray, following the sign for Hawkshead at the junction.

Just a few yards beyond this junction go left along the rough drive signposted for Basecamp, a National Trust training centre. Remain with the drive and pass by the turn to Basecamp on your left. Go through the gate and continue up along the forest road to the sharp left hand bend some fifty or so yards ahead. On the right here look for the stile marked with a white waymark arrow. Go over this and follow the narrow but obvious path up through the trees, soon crossing a small brook.

At the top end of the woods walk ahead to the tall ladder stile (which may have been replaced by a gate by the time you read this), climb this and walk up the long, steady climb up the bracken-covered hillside beyond which will bring you to the summit of Latterbarrow. This modest summit (only 803 feet above sea level), capped by a chimney-like monument offers huge views to all points of the compass including many of the highest peaks in England.

Take your leave of the summit down along the grassy path which heads towards distant Hawkshead church. At the fork just before the fir trees bear right and, on reaching the path in the trees, go right again and descend through the wych elms, keeping the fence to your left and heading virtually for Outgate in the distance. The mountain dominating the horizon ahead of you is Weatherlam, to the north-west of Coniston. At the bottom the path issues onto a minor road. Turn left along this and remain with it for a good half mile, ignoring the turn to Loanthwaite.

In about half a mile go right, down the narrow roadway which leads past Croft Head Cottage on your left. Immediately past this go left into the pull-in which leads to the green-doored garage. To the right of this, and of a field gate, enter the pasture at the waymark arrow. Walk ahead for a few yards to the point where the field opens out. At this point bear half right and head for the short section of wall, at the left hand end of which is a stone step stile.

Cross this and walk directly ahead across the rough pasture in the direction indicated by a waymark arrow. At the far corner of this pasture, below the oak, ash and pine trees is a further stone step stile, beyond which the path falls steeply to a gate. Cross virtually straight over the Green Lane beyond this gate and follow the path through the field beyond to rejoin the path by which you left Hawkshead at the start of the walk. Simply bear left along this to return to the village.

A quiet corner of Hawkshead

18. Barngates

Route: Barngates – Knipe Fold – Arnside Plantation – Bull Close

Distance: 7 miles

Map: O.S. Outdoor Leisure Series Sheet 7; The English Lakes, SE.

Start: The Drunken Duck, Barngates. Grid Reference: NY 352013.

Access: The pub stands at an isolated crossroads high above the western shore of Windermere. From Ambleside take the A593 towards Coniston, forking left at Clappersgate towards Hawkshead. Take the first turn on the right, about 1.5 miles later, and the Drunken Duck is a further mile along this road. From Hawkshead take the B5286 towards Ambleside and fork left opposite the Outgate Inn; the Drunken Duck is at the far end of this narrow road.

The Drunken Duck (09666 347)

From the seats on the grass verge opposite the pub you can watch sunset's hues change the colours of Windermere, far below, from silver through blue to violet and black. Nearer to hand, two small tarns hem in the pubs car parks and trout ripple the surfaces; the view across the top one, reached by a path from the back of the car park, is excellent. The Drunken Duck is one of the Lake District's most famous pubs; it's position and isolation making all the more reason to seek it out. The origin of the idiosyncratic name is explained on a painted board near the one small bar; I'll leave you the pleasure of reading it at your will.

Some fifteen years ago, when I first stopped off here, another reason for searching the place out was Theakston's Old Peculier, then a rare brew on draught, served from a tiny bar the ceiling of which was bedecked with rare and unusual beermats. The mats have gone but the bar and beer remain, supplemented by Theakston's XB, Jennings Bitter, Tetley's Bitter, Marstons Pedigree and Yates Bitter. The tiny bar now is the centre-piece of a much extended business, renowned for its food as much as the range of beers. Off the back of the bar are two small snugs, the long narrow bar room itself being dotted with a few tables, settles and stools. To the left, two larger rooms used largely for dining but open to the drinker to escape the crush at the bar.

From the Drunken Duck, at Barngates, you can watch the sun set over Windermere.

The walls and beams are a jumble of artefacts ranging from old yokes through a considerable collection of mounted antlers/horns to cases of fishing flies. There's a definite hunting theme to many of the line drawings and prints that profuse throughout the pub including a large and whimsical collection by Cecil Aldin dating from 1900. In the bar, an old photograph of the Barngates Inn as was (you can still make out the name on the gable end above the car park) shows how little the low, whitewashed pub has changed externally (at least from the front) this century.

The rose-covered verandah still sports a riot of hanging baskets, only the mode of transport has changed. What has changed is the amount of accommodation available with large extensions at the back and incorporating adjoining cottages. No doubt this is intended for those in search of very comfortable country accommodation, but I couldn't help but think that Victorian landlady who gave the pub its name would smile to read the signwriting outside the pub which advertises "Residential Trout Fishing" – brings to mind a member of the Salmon Family wearing tweeds, smoking a pipe and casting a line into a nearby tarn.......

The pub is open from 11.30-3 and 6-11, food is served between 12-2 and 6.30-9, with more restricted hours on Sundays.

The Walk

Turn left from the pub and immediately left again down the narrow road signposted for Skelwith Bridge. Even in summer this is a quiet by-way, a pleasant stroll alongside hedgerows resplendent in Honeysuckles and Dog Roses, Foxgloves and Wood Crane's Bill. In about half a mile the road bends sharply to the right; at this juncture turn left and climb the stile leading to the woodland road. If you can manage a steep scramble then take a moment to turn right and follow the brook downstream to its confluence with the larger Pull Beck. Here turn left and scramble up the steep slope to reach a vantage point looking up at Pull Force, a relatively little known falls plunging fifty and more feet over two ledges from the heights of Pull Scar en route to Windermere.

Return to the woodland road and follow it alongside the birch and oak woodland. In a short while climb a stile and continue along the track, favouring the left path at a fork. Down to your left a flush of reeds and grasses indicates the presence of a boggy area which remains with you for a considerable distance. Pass through a number of gates, all the while remaining at the bottom edge of the wooded slope, here and there glimpsing the topmost crags of Black Crag up to the right. One field you pass through is particularly rich in Ragged Robin with its distinctive, feathery, pink/red flowers, and Common Spotted-Orchid; the next pasture hosts an overgrown pond rich with lilies, iris and dragonflies.

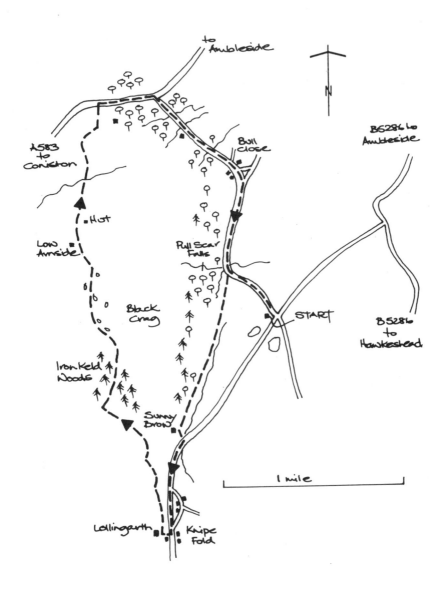

to Ambleside

N

A583 to Coniston

Bull Close

B5286 to Ambleside

Hut

Low Arnside

Pull Scar Falls

Black Crag

Iron Keld Woods

START

B5286 to Hawkeshead

Sunny Brow

1 mile

Lollingarth

Knipe Fold

Go through the gate opposite the cottage and turn left down the rough drive; on reaching the minor road turn right and walk along to the hamlet of Knipe Fold. Ahead, the view extends over the tumble of houses that is Hawkshead to Esthwaite Water. At the fork remain on the upper road and continue until a further road comes in at an obtuse angle from your left. A few yards past this point, and just before reaching the brow of the hill, go right up the narrow lane immediately before a white cottage with a green door. At the top of this short lane, and opposite a house called Lollingarth, turn right along a wider lane, then following this for nearly a mile.

This is an old quarry road and becomes rougher the higher it climbs. It winds through areas of scrubby woodland and veritable forests of Juniper bushes. From several points are excellent views east to Windermere and the high Fells and Pikes of the Fairfield Horseshoe and south-east to Esthwaite Water. After a while the fir plantation of Iron Keld appears on the right, and the track crests the ridge to reveal a superb view across a small tarn to the heights of southern and central Lakeland – Wetherlam, Scafell and Great Gable. Down to the left, you may catch a glimpse of Tarn Hows.

Soon after this little tarn, the woods peel back for a short distance around a sharp crag. At the end of this clearing, on your right, a Bridleway sign points the way along a forest track. Walk up along this, watching for red squirrels which seem surprisingly unperturbed by the passing of ramblers or riders. On sunny days the light filtering down through the firs catches yellow and green lichen growing on tree stumps and boulders, adding a touch of unexpected colour to the rather austere fir woods.

Climb the stile or go through the gate at the end and swing gently left with the main track which starts its descent from the crags of this, Arnside Plantation. Excellent views open out over the Langdale Valleys and to the heights above Grasmere. Simply remain with the track, pass through the gate and keep the wall on your left. In places the surface is boggy and supports small pools, home to Common Butterwort and patrolled by dragonflies. Half a mile's walk will bring you past the isolated farmstead of Lower Arnside, off to your left.

Scafell seen from Iron Keld

The track passes through a gap at the corner of two walls. Walk a few yards further and go to the left of the blue bridleway arrow. A few yards further again an isolated signpost offers a choice of route, select the bridleway option, to the right. The way is indistinct for a while, simply walk through the rocky terrain, keeping the little stone hut well up to your right.

You'll soon catch a glimpse of Elter Water ahead of you, this is the direction in which to walk. The track gradually becomes more obvious once you've passed through a gate in the corner of two pastures. Soon after this ford the stream and continue gradually downhill through the juniper and thorn bushes. The track winds round a small crag and leads down to a road beside a bungalow.

Turn right along this road, which is the A593 and can be busy, but you must follow it for nearly half a mile. The first road on the right, signposted to Hawkshead, is the route to take. In contrast to the main road this is a peaceful lane, rising through pleasant woodlands, crossing beck after beck and lined with walls built with well rounded boulders dripping with wildflowers, ferns and mosses. Bear right at the junction, walk on between the few cottages at Bull Close and bear right again at the next, triangular junction. Less than a mile later, you'll arrive back at the isolated crossroads next to the Drunken Duck.

Nearby Tarn Hows – a renowned beauty spot

19. Dunnerdale

Route: Seathwaite – Tongue House – Birks Bridge – Wallowbarrow Crag

Distance: 6 miles

Map: O.S. Outdoor Leisure Sheet 6, The English Lakes SW.

Start: The Newfield Inn, Seathwaite. Grid Reference: SD 227960

Access: Take the A595 west from Broughton in Furness. In a little over a mile the road reaches the bridge over the River Duddon, a crossing controlled by traffic lights. Immediately before this bridge is a turn to the right, signposted for Ulpha. Take this narrow, winding road and drive to Ulpha, turning right at the junction in this hamlet to follow another narrow road (signposted for Seathwaite and the Wrynose Pass) for a further three miles to arrive at the Newfield Inn.

Parking: Parking at the pub is very restricted and a notice warns you not to park and walk. The landlord, however, was quite happy to let me leave my car in front of the pub **once I'd checked with him**. If you find that you aren't given permission to park there then there are a few parking spaces opposite the chapel, a hundred yards or so north of the pub. The alternative is to park at the Forestry Commission car park near Birks Bridge (about three miles north of the pub) and call in at the Newfield half way round your walk. Please don't just ignore the notice at the pub and park anyway, the tiny parking area also serves the adjoining cottage and flats and is **not** dedicated to the pub.

The Newfield Inn (0229 716208)

There's not much to Seathwaite. A couple of farms, the odd cottage or two, the chapel and a pub strung alongside the ribbon of tarmac that sneaks up the Duddon Valley. What it lacks in size, however, it makes up for in situation; the modest volcanic, slate and limestone crags of Dunnerdale contrive to keep the valley secluded and peaceful, the soils encourage the survival of ancient sessile oak woodlands and produce rich haymeadows a riot of colour in mid and late summer.

The Newfield Inn makes the most of this situation. From the tables on the rear terrace are glorious autumnal views of the bracken-burnished hillsides and the myriad hues of the mixed oak and fir woodlands. The very rocks themselves, too, can appear all colours of the rainbow as the angle of the sun changes.

Inside, the bar floor is testimony to the incredible rock types found in the area. Blocks rather than slabs of slate have been laid on their side to form the floor, thus exposing the distinct layering of the muds, sands and other sediments that fell to the bed of a sea five hundred million years ago, later to be compressed, heated and metamorphosed into the slates that make such an unusual flooring. Occasionally spilt onto this floor may be drops of the Theakstons Best, XB and Old Peculier on offer at the large bar.

The pub itself is capacious. The main bar area is split into three distinct parts, casually furnished with old pews, benches, wall and window seats, bench and trestle tables and a variety of other styles on which to plant both pint and person. The back dining room, open when the pub is busy, has an enormous fireplace all but buried beneath piles of logs put there to dry before being used (Seathwaite is one of the wettest places in England, rainfall in the surrounding fells averages about 150 inches – that's thirteen feet – a year).

The main bar area, a mixture of wood panelling, rough stone and huge old beams, is decorated with a few watercolours, old photographs and maps and with reams of information about local places and events. An age old newspaper cutting records the sorry story of the Seathwaite Riot when workers employed to construct the dam and works associated with Seathwaite Tarn (used to supply water to Barrow in Furness) became somewhat over-excited ("tired and emotional" perhaps?), the local militia were called on to restore order resulting in the death of one worker and the incapacitation of several others.

The pub is open from 11am-3pm and 6pm-11pm, occasionally all day depending on circumstances. Food is available during most of these hours, the helpings are enormous.

The Walk

(This is not a walk for the unadventurous or lily-livered! Two miles into it you have to cross a torrent at a series of waterfalls for which some agility and self-confidence are needed to make the required leap. Further, some stretches will be very boggy in wet weather, so boots are a must. Finally, there are one or two steep scrambles over rough ground to contend with).

Turn right out of the pub and wind with the road for a hundred or so yards to reach Seathwaite Chapel, a squat little place of worship built from local slate several centuries ago. This is where the saintly Reverend Robert Walker preached for the 67 years he was curate, finally dying in 1802 at the age of 93. Because of his charitable acts he was christened "Wonderful Walker," ensured of lasting fame by Wordsworth who based one of his famous Duddon Sonnets around the curate. Outside the porch of the church is the stone used by Walker for clipping sheep on – both he and his wife produced copious amounts of woollen garments that clothed many of the residents of this scattered community. A simple memorial brass to Walker is inside the church; there are also memorials and gravestones to a number of other Walkers, appropriate indeed as the chapel is a favourite stop for walkers in the Dunnerdale Fells!

Regain the road and continue northwards along the narrow valley of this, Tarn Beck. Here and there on your left are cataracts and waterfalls which well repay a slight detour to the riverbank. In about a mile a turn on the right is signposted for "Coniston, unfit for cars." This is the route you should follow. It's the end of the renowned Walna Scar Road, an old pack horse and quarry road leading over to Coniston, a favourite walk of Wordsworth who was a great fan of this south western corner of the Lake District. In a short while bear left at the fork towards Hollin House, leaving the Walna Scar Road to rise to around 2000 feet before descending to Coniston.

Walk on along the tarmaced lane, past Hollin House and alongside the lively little Tarn Beck to reach the white-painted Tongue House Farm. Walk with the lane around the back of the cottage and then turn left in front of the barn, go through the gate and up along the stony field road, following the line of the tumbledown wall on your right. In two

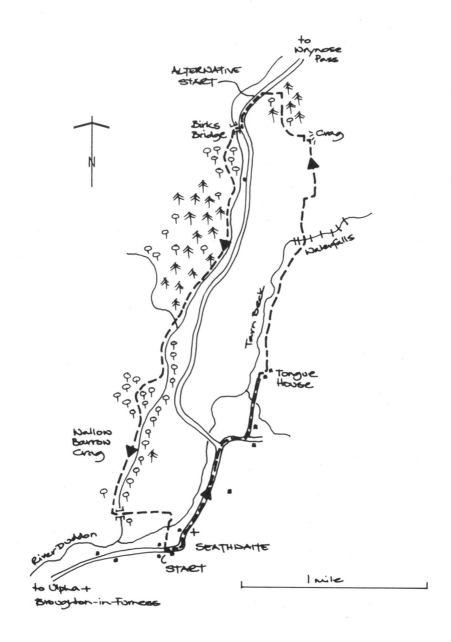

hundred yards or so look on your left for a ladder stile, climb over this and turn right (there's a footbridge down to the left, ignore this).

Tarn Beck plunges down in a spectacular series of waterfalls and shoots

The path is now ill-defined and rather boggy. Just follow Tarn Beck (to your left) upstream, parallelled by a line of telegraph poles. Go through the gap in the wall beside a one of these poles and continue upstream. You'll soon reach a point where Tarn Beck plunges down from your right over a spectacular series of waterfalls and shoots, coursing its way through boulders and pot-holes in a braided defile. You've got to cross these torrents, you can see the route of the path some distance ahead, marked by a ladder stile next to a telegraph pole. I'll leave you to find your own way across, there are places where the defile is little more than a step wide. Take your time to find the most appropriate crossing point, and look for the boot marks of earlier walkers as a clue..

Once across walk up to and climb the ladder stile, then head for the gate in the wall ahead. Fifty yards or so beyond this turn right and walk up the hillside to join the line of wall across the fellside, turning left along this line and keeping the wall to your right, following it virtually to its end at a small crag at the top corner of a fir plantation. This is the highest point you'll reach on the walk. Ahead you may catch sunlight reflecting from a car as it toils up Hard Knott Pass.

To your left the fir plantations of Dunnerdale Forest cloak the southern and eastern lower slopes of Harter Fell; the planters have made an effort to break the monotony by leaving shallow crags and patches of grass free of trees and leaving the top edge rather ragged, a change from the usual geometric precision of such plantations. South is a glorious vista down the Duddon Valley, the rounded, higher slopes of Ulpha Fell, Whitfell and Black Combe to the right contrasting with the craggy heights of the Dunnerdale Fells on your left.

As the path reaches the woodland edge, don't go through the gate at the very top corner. Instead launch yourself down the steep hillside for a few yards, go through the gap in the wall on your right and turn left, walking down the steep path between the wall and the wire fence, beyond which are the trees. At the bottom climb the stile, turn left and follow the line of the wall up into the trees. A fairly obvious path winds steeply up through the trees, once over the crest of the slope bear right with the path away from the wall and continue on through the plantation. When you get to the forestry road turn left and walk down to the minor road, turning left along this. In a few hundred yards the Forestry Commission parking and picnic area at Dunnerdale Forest appears on your right. (This is the alternative place to park and commence the walk from).

Remain with the road for a short distance and then turn right at the public bridleway sign, which turn will bring you to Birks Bridge, an old pack horse bridge arching high above the Duddon. The boggy meadow upstream of this structure is rich in Common Spotted Orchids. Beneath and below the bridge are a spectacular series of pot-holes and water worn rocks, just downstream is Great Wood, a surviving tract of the ancient wildwood. Once across the bridge bear left and favour the permissive path for Seathwaite and Wallowbarrow which crosses a short stretch of boardwalk and then angles up into these woods. As the legend on the sign suggests the riverside path you now follow can be rather difficult underfoot. In about two hundred yards ignore the fork to the right and carry on through the trees. Cross the stile and favour the path which angles up the hillside rather than follow the one along the line of the wall on your left. Walk up over the craggy area and head back down towards the river, re-entering the woods after a short scramble over a small crag. At this point a further permissive path sign confirms you are on the right track, bear left with it and walk on down through the plantation to reach the riverbank. Go through the gap in the wall and walk downstream.

Stretches of boardwalk take you over particularly boggy areas as the path picks a way between the trees and across various side streams and areas of fallen rocks. At the fork continue along the path signposted for Seathwaite and Wallowbarrow. Climb the stile, cross the footbridge over a brook and pick a way across the boggy area beyond. In a short while you'll find a small sign "Advised route, follow line of fence." Do as it suggests and climb up away from the river, emerging some distance later at the top of a high river cliff. Stick with the path and drop back down to the riverside, again following it downstream. The route now darts in and out of the wildwood, and crosses the lower edge of a massive boulder field that marks the foot of Wallowbarrow Crag.

Climb the stone step stile at the far side of these boulders and walk along to the solid slate footbridge over the Duddon. Cross this, which was built by W. Grizenthwaite in 1934, then follow the path straight ahead of you, a wall on your right. The path soon leaves the woods and Seathwaite is visible in the distance. Cross the mill leat and, a few yards later the wooden footbridge over Tarn Beck, then follow the path across the meadow and pass through the field gates beside the farm to reach The Inn.

The old packhorse bridge, over the Duddon.

20. Cartmel & Hampsfield Fell

Route: Cartmel – Hampsfield Fell – Hampsfield Hall – Aynsome Mill

Distance: 4.5 miles

Map: O.S. Pathfinder Sheets 626 (Broughton in Furness) & 636 (Grange over Sands.

Start: The King's Arms, Cartmel. Grid Reference: SD 378787.

Access: Cartmel is two miles west of Grange over Sands and is signposted (rather poorly) from the centre of Grange. If approaching from the north, Cartmel can be approached via several minor roads which head south from the A590, just look for the brown road signs indicating Cartmel Priory.

The King's Arms (05395 36220)

The King's Arms is an imposing old pub forming one side of the tiny village square virtually by itself. At the height of summer the pub almost disappears behind myriad hanging baskets, window boxes and the flower tubs which dot the cobbled square in front of this Whitbread house. Here there are a few tables and benches at which to sit and enjoy the Castle Eden or Flowers IPA on offer at the long, solid, wooden bar.

There's a large, open plan interior divided into distinct sections by solid oak pillars and panels. Massive dark oak beams criss cross the low ceiling whilst the walls host a smattering of watercolours of local scenes, a large collection of brass oddments and a miners lamp or two; also displayed are copies of the pub licences dating from the 1850's. A mixture of wall and window seats, benches, pews and chairs crowd this comfortably furnished main room. A pool table takes up much of the room in the semi-panelled back room whilst a side room directly off the main area acts as a kind of snug. One unfortunate trait is the "Elevator Muzak" which detracts from the obvious charm of this long established village local. The King's Arms is open all day (11am-11pm) Mondays to Saturdays and standard Sunday hours.

Cartmel

Cartmel is an enigma. It's just far enough off the traditional "beaten track" around the Lake District to remain unspoiled, and yet is sufficiently well known not to qualify as "undiscovered." This leaves the village in the happy position of being uncluttered for much of the year. All the more surprising, then, that one of England's architectural and historical gems is the focal point of this ancient village in the valley of the River Eea. The parish church of St. Mary and St. Michael survived intact the dissolution of its Augustinian Priory in the reign of Henry 8th and can thus claim to be one of the handful of such buildings in the country with a continual history of worship since its foundation (in this case, 1188).

As the church of a major Priory its size is out of all proportion to the village it serves. The massive, airy interior houses many interesting and unusual tombs, look for the Harrington effigy tomb and, high on one wall, a memorial dated 30 February! The carved oak wood of the fifteenth century screen and the misericords is amongst the finest to be found anywhere. Both inside and outside are memorials to travellers who perished whilst attempting to cross the treacherous sands between Morecambe and the Cartmel Peninsular; the Black Friars used to act as guides across these sands but, despite this, there were many fatalities.

The village itself is little more than a huddle of winding streets in the shadow of the church, radiating from the compact village square resplendent with the village pump beside the market cross. Old coaching inns and tiny cottages are pre-dated by the old Priory Gatehouse on Cavendish Street, now owned by the National Trust but once the village grammar school. To the west of the village is the race-course, used on three or four occasions a year when, unless you're a racing fan, the area is best avoided.

The Walk

Leave the tiny square in the centre of Cartmel, pass under the old gateway arch and follow the narrow, winding road around the northern

map 21

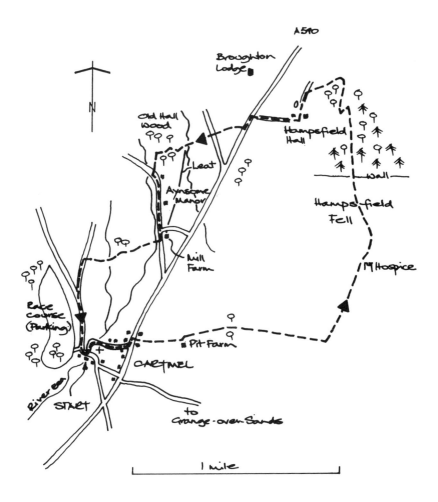

side of the village and the Priory grounds. At the end turn left along the more major road and walk along for about thirty yards, then look on the right for a public footpath sign for "Hospice of Hampsfell", the sign being partially obscured by a laurel bush. Hampsfell is a corruption of Hampsfield Fell. Walk up the steps here and along the narrow path to its end. Pass through the gate at this point and then follow the line of the hedge on your right up across the field to the farm buildings.

On reaching the top end of the field go through the gate (slightly offset from the corner) and go left a few paces along the drive leading away from Pit Farm. Bear right around the end of the new slurry pit and walk up into the field to the left of the large black coloured barn. Set your sights on the top left corner of this massive field and commence the long, steady climb up the fellside.

There's a public footpath sign a few yards from this corner and along the top wall. Go through the gate here and continue uphill, sticking to the line of the wall on your left. At the top end of this pasture tackle the kissing gate and pause to take in the views which already include, to the north and west, many of the highest of Lakeland's mountains. Take a bearing up the steep fellside ahead to the anchor-pylon at the end of the line of electricity pylons and follow the wide path up through the bracken and scrubby thorn trees along this line of sight. Pass by this last pylon some yards to your left and continue up the slope to the ridge top.

Here, views open out over the wide sands of the Kent Estuary to the Pennines, a great black wall forming a continual horizon some fifteen miles to the east. Forming the far shore of the estuary are the wooded, craggy limestone knolls at Warton, Silverdale and Arnside, largely an AONB and/or Nature Reserve belonging to the RSPB. You may well spot the odd tractor or Landrover on the sands at low tide, some locals still gather cockles and other shellfish continuing a practice dating back thousands of years.

Turn left along the crest of the ridge and follow the well-defined path gently uphill, the peculiar squat tower of Hampsfell Hospice soon coming into view. This is your target, so clamber up the shallow, natural limestone steps to reach the edifice. It was provided by a local benefactor, G Remington, in 1846, a man who certainly left his mark at this windy spot. Inside the Hospice are a number of boards recording in whimsical rhymes the reasons this Victorian walker provided the shelter.

The beauty of the Hospice's site is best appreciated from it's parapets, so climb the steep block-steps on the northern side. Without doubt, unless you scale the highest peaks, this is the best place to enjoy a panorama of most of North West England. To the east, Ingleborough stands sharply out from the Pennines; north, the bulk of Helvellyn and glimpses of distant Skiddaw; sweeping west the famous outline of the Langdale Pikes lead to Bowfell and Scafell. The view south is over the glistening sands of Morecambe Bay; the distinct, wooded headland near to hand is Humphrey Head, further west (right) is the long, low curve of Walney Island.

To help you make the most of this stunning panorama is a variation on a toposcope, or view-finder. Simply swivel the horizontally pivoted arrow to point at a particular peak or pass, read the directional bearing off the scale around the circumference of the host-plane and then refer to the chart attached to the guard rail. Bearing 337, for example, should have you looking at the Langdale Pikes. It's comprehensive enough to give the casual walker and visitor a fascinating glimpse across the very roof of England.

Don't let the enormity of the views here rob you of the beauties spread at – indeed beneath – your feet. The top of Hampsfield Fell is an excellent example of a limestone pavement. Climb onto the area of bare limestone just a few yards to the northeast of the Hospice tower. Here are several acres of fissured limestone rich in the specialized plants which thrive on calcareous deposits. Deep in the fissures (grikes), which can be over six feet deep, are mosses and ferns, cinquefoil and hawkbit whilst scrub sycamore, ash and hawthorn make the best of threadbare soil.

Scramble down from the pavement and walk northwards, very gradually falling away to the left of the ridgetop. You'll soon reach a high limestone-block wall cutting across the ridge. Look for the stile beside a barbed-wire encrusted gate and climb this, then following the obvious path into a plantation of young conifers. The line of trees is continual on your right, patchy on your left; remain with the path and gradually walk downhill at a shallow angle. The lush valley of the little

River Eea to your left, contrasting sharply with the crinkly heights of Newton Fell (ahead) and Ellerside, is dotted with large farmhouses and old halls; the tiny village in the middle distance is Field Broughton.

Pass between two great boulders of limestone and zigzag around with the path, soon joining the line of a wall on your left. Simply remain with this to reach a gate at the bottom of the wood and rough pasture. Go through this gate and keep the coppiced hazel woods immediately to your left. Pass through a further gate and then walk down across the pasture, aiming for the far left hand corner where a gap stile gives access to a farm road. Walk ahead with this and bear left, passing a farm pond on your right. Just before the end of the track go through the left hand, nearer, gate and walk through the farmyard past the small stable block. Pass by the old Hampsfield Hall to your left and then swing right past the final barn, following the farm drive down to the road.

Turn left, and in a matter of yards the driveway to Broughton Lodge sweeps away to the right through a set of gate pillars. Immediately to the left of the pillars a (wooden) footpath sign points into the meadow. Take this path and follow the line of wall, then hedge on your right. Cross straight over the narrow road at the far end and continue through the next meadow, hedge on your right. To your left the bulk of the Priory Church rises like a bastion from a sea of haymeadows, glorious in early/mid summer before the first cutting of this rich fodder. Swing left at the corner, cross the stone slab footbridge and pass through the gap stile, then again keeping the hedge on your right. Climb the stone stile at the end and then another slab bridge, here at the point where a mill leat (which you cross on the slab) leaves the stream.

Walk straight ahead over the meadow and go into the wood at the far side. Initially there's no obvious path, but you soon reach a clearing from which a path leads off to the left. Follow this through the small wood, ignoring the fork to the left which leads to a field gate. A few paces after this, however, as the path bends right, look to your left to find a stone stile protected by a solid mesh fence; climb over this and turn left, following the hedgerow along to a gap stile beside a gate, once through which bear left along the road.

Pass by Aynsome Manor Park Hotel on your left, the house dated 1842, and continue along to the old Mill Farm also on your left. Walk to the far end of the buildings and you'll find the site of the old wheel, mounted above road level and once fed by the leat you crossed a few minutes before. Directly opposite this a small wooden gate gives access to a pasture dominated by an enormous horse chestnut tree. Cross the stream on the slab bridge and then stick with the line of hedge on your left. Go through the gate at the end and continue ahead, a wooded knoll on your right. Bear right beneath the large sycamore at the end of the field and then cross the stream (either ford it or use the stone slab some yards off to the right). Walk directly across the field ahead to the silver birch trees in the corner and join the minor road here, turning left to walk the remaining half mile back to Cartmel, passing the race-course en route.

21. Humphrey Head

Route: Allithwaite – Wyke Farm – Humphrey Head

Distance: 4.5 miles

Map: Sheet SD 37/47 (636) Grange-over-Sands.

Start: The Guide Over Sands, Allithwaite. Grid Reference: SD 386764.

Access: Take the B5277 road from Grange-over-Sands towards Flook-borough and Cark. The pub is on your left at a sharp left hand bend as the road reaches Allithwaite village, about two miles south-west of Grange.

The Guide Over Sands (05395 32438)

"The Square" in Allithwaite is little more than a bend in the B5277 road. There are a few cottages on the north side, but most of the village lies along minor roads just off this main road. Nestled in the tuck of the bend, however, is one of the village's two pubs, the Guide Over Sands. This obscure name will mean absolutely nothing to you until it is put into the context of the local network of roads and tracks which has developed over the centuries.

Since Roman times, and possibly earlier, a routeway has existed across this top corner of Morecambe Bay, saving upwards of 20 miles on the "dry land" route between Lancaster and Cartmel. The route across the sands is a dangerous passage, prone to changes of river channels, quicksand and sandbanks. The Prior of Cartmel Priory used to employ professional guides to ensure that officials, merchants and travellers could travel in relative safety to and from that great ecclesiastic centre; following the dissolution the Crown guaranteed the continuance of this service.

For many decades the Carter family were the official Guides over the sands; from around 1811 they were based at the Royal Oak pub in Allithwaite, later renamed the Guide Over Sands. A comprehensive history of the pub and the job of Guiding is on display in the pub, although the current Guide, Cedric Robinson, lives on a farm at nearby Grange over Sands.

The pub itself is a Whitbread house and displays all the hallmarks of that brewery's idea of a traditional family pub. There are shelves full of old books purchased by the yard/ton, stuffed animals, beams and leaded glass in cornices above the bar; in short their own rather overstated house style of the late 'Eighties. Such personal prejudice apart, however, the range of Whitbread based beers is well looked after, particularly the Castle Eden (there's also Boddingtons and Trophy on handpump). The pub is popular as a place for eating out; there's a large dining area on a sort of mezzanine level at the back end of the bar. The "Guide" is open all day and children are welcome.

The Walk

(This is a gentle, easy walk but one short stretch alongside a seamarsh may be boggy, so boots are probably the best bet for footwear).

From the Guide over Sands turn left and walk down the winding hill until you reach The Pheasant Inn. Turn left here along Jack Lane and then, opposite the pub car park entrance, branch right down the farm drive at the public footpath sign to Wyke House. Walk down through the farmyard and go through the gate into the field at the far end. Follow the partially surfaced field road along the left of this field. A few yards before this track peters out at the site of a field gate (i.e. a gate-sized gap in the hedge...) at the end of the next field look half right to find a stone gap-stile through the hedge to your right. Go through this and then follow the hedgerow on your left to a further gap stile.

Once through this stile walk to the far left hand corner of the field (you're in the correct field if there is some iron rail fencing to your left, surrounding what is marked on old maps as the village sewage works) and cross a small footbridge over a drainage ditch. A further ditch now develops on your left; this is your guide for the next half mile or so, simply keep it to your left and cross stiles, tracks and gates as necessary (including the road to the new works). The high, wooded promontory to

map 22

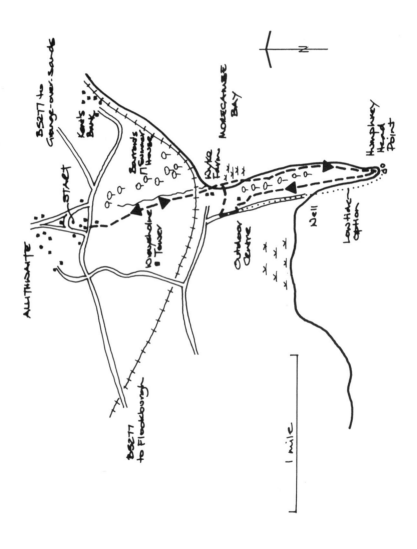

your left is Kirkhead, capped by a monument known as Borrow's Summer House, named after a local dignitary from nearby Grange.

Upon reaching the embankment which carries the Cumbrian Coast Railway across the seamarsh walk under the low, gated underpass and continue along the short sea wall to Wyke Farm. Go through the tiny gate in the wall and then almost immediately climb down the block-steps on your left to gain the foreshore. Turn right and walk along the edge of this vast area of marsh and sandbanks, passing by the farmhouse to your right.

In a hundred yards or so you'll come to a footpath sign atop a pole on the edge of the marsh. If the marsh is proving to be too wet for your liking then you should turn right at this juncture and walk along the path which winds between high hedgerows and below the wooden buildings of a Field Centre owned by North Yorkshire County Council. On reaching the minor road turn left and left again a matter of yards further on up the approach road to the field centre. Turn right into the pasture before you reach the compound and work up the gentle hillside until you see the woods to your left. Walk to the woods and follow the footpath just inside the trees to a point just a few yards from the foreshore. Here, turn right to join the route of the walk outlined.

Those keen to remain on the marsh edge should first estimate roughly where the main area of woodland comes down to the shoreline. With this in mind continue along the marsh edge for about three hundred yards, then keep your eyes peeled for the narrow footpath which angles gently up into the trees. It's marked by an old stone gatepost, painted white years ago but now weathered and well hidden in the undergrowth, and is the point where the woodland meets the foreshore.

Once on this path remain with the route which keeps close company with the rocky shore; the alternative route outlined above almost immediately joins from the right. Wind with the path, narrow but well used, through the mature oak woodland which clothes this leeward side of Humphrey Head. This offers picturesque views across the Kent Estuary to Silverdale, Arnside and the looming bulk of the Pennines beyond – look out for the distinctive shape of Ingleborough. This path eventually emerges from the woods at a stile; climb this and remain with the low cliffline to reach Humphrey Head Point a quarter of a mile or so later.

Humphrey Head

This isolated, near-island belongs to the same geological period and rock type that forms the Yorkshire Dales, Mountain Limestone deposited in a warm tropical sea around 300 million years ago during Carboniferous times. Other outliers of this great system occur all along the southern coast of Cumbria – Arnside Knott or the hills above Barrow for example. At Humphrey Head this limestone has been folded or tilted sharply towards the east. The thrift covered jagged rocks that hold the rock pools at the Point dip steeply into the sands and, looking back to the Head from these pools, the very obvious effect that geology has on the landscape is well demonstrated; the steep cliffs on the western side contrasting sharply with the low cliffs to the east where the rock sinks gently beneath the sands as the rock dips ever steeper.

The cliffs of the western side rise sheer for about 150 feet, eroded here and there where bands of weaker rock have succumbed; at one point a natural arch in the limestone is visible toward the top of the cliff. There are a few springs along this side, the water from one of which was once held to have miraculous curative properties and is known as Holy Well, evidence that monks from Cartmel once used the water. A more poignant claim often associated with Humphrey Head is that it was here, on an indeterminable date, that the last wolf in England was hunted down and killed. Virtually the whole of the headland is designated an Access Area so you can wander at will (except in the grounds of the Field Studies Centre).

Returning inland from the Point you have two choices. If the tide is ebbing then you can walk along the sands beneath the western cliffs. This will bring you to the end of a tarmac road that snakes along the foot of the headland. Walk up along this road to reach the entrance to the access road to the Field Studies Centre.

If, however, you prefer to take in the excellent views from the summit then return to the fence above the rock pools, climb the stile and walk uphill with the fence to your left. In a few hundred yards you'll reach the triangulation pillar at the highest point on the Head, about 173 feet above sea level. From this modest height are superb views west across Furness, east and south to the Forest of Bowland, the Pennines and across the immense sandbanks of Morecambe Bay. To the north you may catch glimpses of some of the lower fells of the Lake District.

The only farm to be seen on the low lying moss area is Wraysholme Tower. This is an excellent example of a Pele Tower, built perhaps seven centuries ago as a place of refuge from incursions by the Scots. (You can, if you wish, walk back to Allithwaite along the narrow roads across the moss and pass close to the Tower. The Tower was once home to the Harrington family, a member of which is said to have been responsible for dispatching the last wolf. Coincidentally, a family member is also credited with killing the Country's last wild boar. Perhaps they were capped by England as huntsmen. The roads, however, have tall hedges so you wouldn't see much else.)

Continue northwards from the pillar and you'll eventually reach the access road to the Field Studies Centre. Turn left along this to the minor road and turn right. Walk a few yards up the road to the end of the old, overgrown lane on your right. Walking up along this will bring you to the edge of the marshes passed earlier in the walk. Turn left here and reverse your earlier route past Wyke Farm and back to Allithwaite.

22. Tarn Hows

Route: Coniston – Low Yewdale – Tarn Hows – Boon Crag

Distance: 5 miles

Map: O.S. Outdoor Leisure Series Sheet 7, The English Lakes, SE.

Start: The Crown Inn, Coniston. Grid Reference: SD 303976.

Access: Coniston lies at the north-western tip of the lake from which it takes it's name. The Crown Hotel and Inn are at the village centre; there is a large pay-car park virtually opposite, the pub has a dedicated car park and on-street parking is permissible between October and March.

The Crown Inn (05394 41243)

One of the focal points of Coniston, The Crown Hotel is a solid, white painted establishment on the road to Hawkshead. There are two distinct drinking areas, the most convivial being the small public bar at the front, a jumble of old beams, wooden chairs and tables; the larger lounge bar is rather more spartan and with a handful of fruit machines. Common to both rooms are stretches of wood panelling and walls liberally dotted with old photographs, prints and paintings of the Coniston of days gone by.

There's a furnace-like open fire to dry off wet or warm up cold extremities, a task also more than adequately carried out by the Robinson's Old Tom, a "falling-down" strength barley wine here, unusually, dispensed by handpump. The other beers are Robinson's Best Bitter and Hartley's XB, all served from a cellar which has won second place in Hartley's "Best Kept Cellar" competition for the very friendly landlord. There's an extensive bar meals menu which is, in common with the beers, available all day.

Coniston

Coniston was a favourite resort of the Victorians, but one largely eclipsed by the rather brasher, larger and more accessible townships of Windermere and Bowness. This geographical fortune means that Coniston remains a small, rather demure town, as close to it's long industrial past as to its Victorian heyday. The steam-yacht Gondola, launched in 1859 and the last survivor of a small fleet of such craft, recalls the days when the lure of John Ruskin's name – he lived at Brantwood, a mansion above the eastern shore of the Lake – ensured profitable trade for local hoteliers catering for the "arty" set of late Victorian England. Ruskin is also remembered by a small museum in the town, the exhibits in which include fine lacework – he is credited with introducing lacemaking to the town after becoming enamoured with the practice whilst in Greece.

But this early tourism was a boon; the foundations of Coniston's history and fortune lie squarely in the local geology. Some commentators suggest a pre-Roman age for some workings, but it was these Latins who first developed the copper mining industry on any scale in the area. The Dark and Middle Ages saw continual, if slow growth, but from the 1600's the activity increased until well over 1000 were employed in the mines up along Church Beck to the west of the village – "Coppermines Valley." This industry brought money and some early luxuries to the town, a small hydro-electricity generator associated with the works also supplied power to the town, one of the earliest to be so-lit in the country.

Some copper ore was smelted in the area using locally produced charcoal but much was exported. Until the mid-Nineteenth century Coniston was a thriving small port, boats running down the lake to its southern tip at Nibthwaite, the ore being transferred here to waggons for the short trip the coastal port of Greenodd, thence to tin-plate works in South Wales and the Bristol Channel area. The branch railway between Coniston and the main coastal line at Foxfield was constructed primarily to take over and speed this trade. All the works are now long-abandoned, as are the slate quarries that not only provided the building materials for the town itself but also sought at one time to rival the North Wales roof-slate industry; Coniston slate is Greenslate rather than the black slates of Ffestiniog. They all look the same in the rain, though. The railway was closed in 1958.

Apart from Windermere, (where the practice may soon be prohibited), Coniston is the only lake in the Lake District where powerboating is, on rare occasions, permitted. This is a hang over from the times when the father and son Campbell team established world speed records on water; the son, Donald Campbell, was killed when his boat, Bluebird, flipped whilst travelling at nearly 300mph in January 1967.

The Walk

Turn left out of the pub and walk down the main road for about 300 yards to the junction immediately before the bridge across Yewdale Beck. Turn left here (signposted for Ambleside) and follow the road alongside the Beck. Ignore the wooden footbridge on your right after about 200 yards, instead continuing a short distance further to find the solid, slate-built Shepherd Bridge over the Beck. Cross this and, at the far side, climb over the step stile on the left and walk the few yards to the wooden stile. Once over this walk up the pasture to the line of oak trees and walk up beside these, a fence on your left. At the top end of the pasture is a peculiar folly-like structure, evidently the remains of a barn of sorts. Pass through the kissing gate to the left of this and continue up the hillside. From here are excellent views west (left) to Coniston Old Man and, nearer to hand, Yew Pike; behind you the long ribbon of Coniston Water snakes southwards through the low lying Furness Fells.

Go through the next gate and follow the path up along the "valley" between ridges of gorse. At the top of the field climb the stiles into and out of the small glade of yew trees. This seems well tended and the stone walls in an excellent state of repair, as if some kind of memorial or burial area, but I found no such supporting evidence. Continue through the woods beyond, leaving by the stile at the far end. To the left are excellent views across to Yewdale and Mart Crags, separated by the torrent of White Gill. The well established old pathway, slabbed in a few places, contours the hillside for a short while; leave it at the waymark arrow and cut across the field, following the path beneath isolated oaks and into the next field. There are extensive views ahead up the valley of

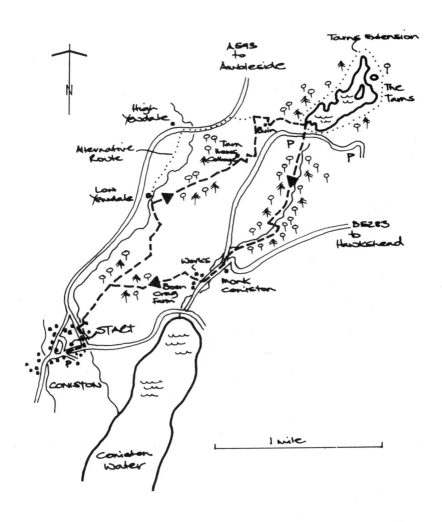

the Yewdale Beck and over lower fells to the Fairfield Horseshoe and Hart Crag, high above Ambleside. Closer to hand the ridge of Holme Fell is feathered by lone rowan trees on many of its' individual crags.

At the end of this next field climb the gate beneath the oaks and bear left along the old quarry road. This winds alongside Yewdale Beck for a short distance to reach a somewhat ornate bridge. Don't cross this with the track, instead climb the stile beneath the yew on your right and walk along the field edge, an unofficial* but well trodden path, to a further stile at the far corner which brings you into the bottom end of Tarn Hows Wood, a large area of National Trust woodland. The track up into the woods is at first narrow but gradually widens out as you gain height. This lower end of the woods has been largely coppiced, but evidently has also suffered in recent gales. Cross the log footbridge over the brook and continue uphill. On reaching the locked gates leading into a fenced enclosure, look for the path just to the left (there's a small footpath sign) and follow this uphill alongside the fence.

After about 200 yards bear off left with the main path, leaving the fenced plantation behind and follow the wide track up to the edge of the woods. Join the line of a wall on your left for a short while – you should pick out the tiny Yew Tree Tarn in the valley below, off to your left is the great wall that is Wetherlam – before re-entering the woods for a few yards to end up at a gate beneath an enormous Ash tree. Look carefully at the hollow created when a lower branch was once lopped and you'll see a holly bush growing out of the Ash tree.

Go through the gate and walk up to the roadway in front of the solid old Tarn Hows Cottage, turn right through the gate here and wind up with the driveway to the gate at the end leading onto a minor road.

---

*NOTE: Should it prove impractical to use this access to the N.T. woods, then cross the ornate bridge over Yewdale Beck at this point and walk the few yards up to the farm. Immediately before reaching such go right at the footpath sign and walk along, soon joining the line of a wall on your right. Remain with this obvious path through several pastures to reach the main road opposite High Yewdale. Turn right along the road and follow it to the sharp left hand bend nearly half a mile distant. Here, take the bridleway on the right and walk up this to find the gate beneath the large spruce, then following the directions from that point as outlined in the text.

You can, if you wish, walk left up the tarmaced road here to reach the Tarns but I chose to stay with footpaths. To do so turn sharp left and walk down the rough track beside the wall. In a few hundred yards pass through an old gateway, soon after this look on your right for a field gate beneath a large spruce. Go through this and along the field road beyond. Ford the shallow stream and look to the hillside ahead. You need to walk left along the upper of the two tracks which cut across the hillside, so walk to the old enclosure and ruined barn and pick up this upper track here. Follow it up to the trees, hairpin right with it at the corner of the woods and walk up to the gate at the top corner. Once through this go straight ahead along the path up through the bracken, eventually ending up at the famous beauty spot of Tarn Hows.

Tarn Hows refers to the series of crinkly crags which surround the water, Hows being a corruption of hills. The Tarn itself was once a string of small pools and swampy hollows, transformed into the one stretch of water seen today last century. The area was presented to the National Trust in 1930 as a memorial to local notaries Sir James and Lady Anne Scott. On a summer weekend it can be horribly crowded here as it is one of the Lake District's most renowned, and accessible, viewpoints; so much so, in fact, that the access roads are all one way to ease congestion. By the same token, however, once you leave the immediate vicinity of the Tarn and car parks you can soon lose the crowds.

There's a well marked and used path that circles the Tarn, particularly pleasant in the autumn when the trees are turning. This circuit would add about two miles and half an hour to your walk should you undertake it. Just turn left as you get to the water and walk clockwise around the Tarn.

To return to Coniston, go to the westernmost car park (the one without the conveniences, some yards to the right of the point where you first reach the Tarn). Immediately to the left of this (as you look at it from the road) a forestry road cuts ahead and gradually downhill into the woodland. Follow this track to the point where it hairpins to the left, at which point continue straight ahead along the lesser-used track. Down to your left a stream tumbles noisily along a narrow, deep valley. Look out here for red squirrels, surprisingly plentiful if you pause for a few minutes and keep eyes peeled and ears alert.

At the T-junction at the end of this track turn left, wind down with the forest road and cross the stream. Walk up to the junction and turn right, then remain with this roadway for the next half mile to reach a minor road. Here and there beside the road are small, artificial ponds, marked by distinctive vegetation such as yellow iris, presumably associated with undertakings once carried out by monks once based at Monk Coniston, some way down the road.

On reaching the minor road turn left, cross the stream and walk up to the more major road, bearing right along this. In about three hundred yards go right, into the yard beside the post box and signposted to Boon Crag Farm. Walk up past the woodyard on your right and past the farm itself, a few yards further on. At the right hand bend, marked by a loading ramp built of sleepers and slate, go over the stile beside the gate on your left and follow the old field road up along the line of trees.

Enter the woods via the gate and continue along the track to the signpost pointing to the route of a "Permitted path to Coniston." Bear right with this and follow the markers – short poles with a white top – up through the woods. The highest part of this plantation is of pine trees, beyond which the path falls steeply down to a stile beneath a huge Spanish chestnut. Climb the stile and walk straight ahead over the low, gorse covered ridge. In the dip beyond this turn left along the path and retrace your steps back into Coniston.

23. Bouth

Route: Bouth – Low Hay Bridge – Rusland – Oxen Park

Distance: 7.5 miles

Map: O.S. Pathfinder Series Sheet 626, Broughton in Furness.

Start: The White Hart, Bouth, nr. Newby Bridge. Grid Reference: SD 328856.

Access: Bouth is a compact little village lying about one mile to the north of the A590 road. From Newby Bridge drive towards Barrow along the A590. Once past the station and steam centre at Haverthwaite look for the signpost for Bouth, to your right, and follow the subsequent signs to the village. The pub is in the centre a few yards along the road towards Oxen Park and Force Forge.

The White Hart (0229 861229)

Bouth is little more than a hamlet, tucked away in a wide, shallow valley in the Furness Fells a few miles south of Grizedale Forest. Hard to imagine that this peaceful place, past winner of the regional "Best Kept Small Village" title, was once nicknamed "L'il Hell." It was, it seems, a favoured watering place for the dockers and sailors from the small port of Greenodd, a couple of miles to the south, a busy little place exporting wool, slate and copper. They tended to enjoy a glass or two at the surprisingly large number of ale-houses and inns that Bouth once supported and were men of few words and many fists. There was a saying in Furness that it "used to take four days to get through Bouth." Whether this was because of injuries sustained in brawls or the lure of the beer is hard to say.

The White Hart is the sole survivor of the inns from those days of yore. It began life as a coaching inn in the 1600's, custom in later centuries included market traders (the village held a market until Victorian times) and charcoal burners (the last recorded burners worked at nearby Ealinghearth until just before the Second war). The long, low, whitewashed building is resplendent with colourful window-boxes throughout the summer, the entrance porch an archway of climbing roses. Inside, the one large, partially panelled room is rather dimly illuminated by two small-paned bow windows, a light source that makes the most of the mixed decoration within. The local taxidermist must have made a fortune here, in one corner of the bar every wallspace, nook and cranny is home to stoat, weasel, pike, mink or fox. Other nails and hooks support old peat-cutting tools, a collection of clay pipes and a display of cask plugs. To the right as you go in is an evocative collection of old photographs of the village.

The old settles, window seats and tables look as if they've survived from coaching days; the two great fireplaces probably consume as much wood during the winter as the charcoal burners once did. The discerning reader will be delighted by a glance at the substantial wooden bar, home to handpumps offering Tetley Bitter, Arrol's Eighty 'Bob, Hartleys XB, Ind Coope Burton and Greenalls Original; soon to be added is Boddingtons and guest beers include Mitchells and Jennings.

There's a large games room set well apart from the bar area and at the rear of the pub a few seats on a terrace which looks out across lush meadows to the thick woodlands above the Old Hall. Opening hours are noon-3pm, and 6-11pm on Mondays to Wednesdays, 11am-11pm Thursdays to Saturdays and standard Sunday hours. Bar meals are available from 12-2pm and 7-8.30pm (possibly excluding Tuesdays) and you can stay at the White Hart if you fancy a few days away from it all.

The Walk

Turn left from the pub and follow the lane which winds along just above the floor of the valley, passing by a number of old cottages and yeomans houses. At the junction where this lane bends sharply left, continue straight ahead along the lane signposted for "Hay Bridge only," shortly walking past a small bus garage. Simply remain with this lane for something over a mile. The views of the well wooded Furness Fells are excellent, look out also for a good count of buzzard, kestrel, sparrowhawk and little owls quartering the rough pastures hereabouts.

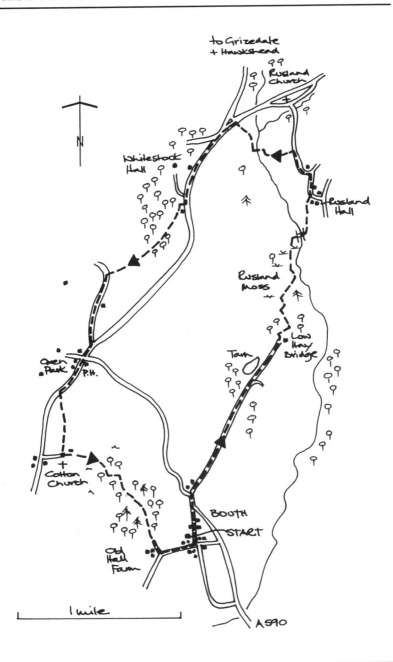

About half way along the lane you'll enter the Haybridge Nature
Reserve. As the sign requests, stick to the right of way which is the lane.
Keep left at the fork soon passing by a tranquil tarn off to your left.
Beyond this the green of Grizedale Forest cloaks the low fells and
forming the horizon are the high mountains beyond Ambleside. The lane
eventually reaches Low Hay Bridge, the home of the Hay Bridge Deer
Museum and Nature Reserve, established in 1971 by a former chief game
warden of Grizedale Forest, Herbert Fooks, to protect the habitat of red
and roe deer. It's more of an educational/training centre for those
interested in deer management and conservation than a visitor facility
per se, although you can visit the centre (telephone 0229 861412).

The route of the walk continues through the Nature Reserve. At the
entrance to the small car park is a tiny footpath sign on your right,
directing you right towards Rusland. So turn right beside the gatepost
and walk down through the woods, cross the rough roadway at the
bottom and walk ahead to the footbridge which, as the sign indicates,
marks the boundary of a wildlife sanctuary. Once across the bridge stay
with the narrow path, marked here and there by white-topped posts and
wind out onto the area of mossland that is Rusland Moss Site of Special
Scientific Interest. Its an unexpected, rather eerie landscape, dotted with
dwarf birch trees and the occasional stand of scots pine, thick with low
bushes, heather, bracken and reedbeds. Stand still for a few moments
and you'll hear loud crashings from within the trees and reeds, splashes
from hidden ponds and drainage ditches which flow lazily into the river,
named here as Rusland Pool. Evidence of deer, otter and red squirrels?
It's impossible to say.

At a couple of points the path comes suddenly on narrow log
footbridges with a guard rail on one side only, so don't walk too quickly
unless you fancy an unplanned dip. Eventually the path reaches the
edge of a further drainage ditch, turn left with the path and follow it
through the head-high rushes. There are also a lot of wildflowers here in
summer – Ragged Robin, Forget me not, Iris and Yellow Rattle for
example. A couple of hundred yards will find you on a short causeway
leading to an old bridge, once over which you should wind up with the
track to emerge in the hamlet of Rusland. A major attraction here is
Rusland Hall which has a renowned collection of self-playing musical
instruments (eg. grand pianos and pianolas) and very rare white
peacocks.

As you get to the top of the rough track at the corner beside the Gate House turn left and walk down the minor road, bearing left in front of the cottages which house the Forest Spinners Craft Centre. About a hundred yards past these cottages, as the road bends right, look on the left for a rough lane and walk along this to a large rough clearing, beyond which cross the little metal footbridge over the beck. Walk ahead from this to the kissing gate and once through this turn right. Look to your right across the beck here to find Rusland Church, isolated on a small crag; the novelist Arthur Ransome (Swallows and Amazons) is buried here.

At the end of the field go through the kissing gate beside the field gate and turn left along the track, bearing left again at the fork and following this narrower path along to the road junction. Bear left here and, shortly, left again towards Oxen Park. Remain with this minor road for a good half mile, eventually passing by the entrance to the driveway which curves across the fields to the imposing Whitestock Hall. On your right a short distance after this, and as the road bends left, is a pull-in area with a gate at the rear. Go through this gate and turn left, walking up the steep pasture and behind the houses down to your left.

At the top-left corner of the pasture go through the rickety kissing gate which gives access to a woodside track, walk up along this, the woods on your right and a wall and steep field to your left. Leave the area of woodland via the gate and continue along the field track beyond. Pass through the next gate and walk up the rough pasture, keeping initially a fence and then the woodland edge close to your right. In 200 yards or so enter the woods via the gate at the corner and follow the path up through these woods, keeping the wall close on your left. Leave the woods again at the top end and walk straight ahead up through the rough pasture, aiming for and passing by the stunted oak tree. Pass the old sheep pens, go through the gate and go virtually straight ahead along the rough farm road.

At the end of this road turn right to reach the hamlet of Oxen Park, centred around the old Manor House which is now the pub (Hartleys, bar meals). The settlement's name derives from the use made of the area by the monks of Furness Abbey who raised and grazed these valuable beasts on the rich upland haymeadows. Besides the pub there are a few old cottages (the one near the pub, for example, has a lavish masons mark, more of a datestone, dated 1697), farms and smallholdings hidden in the folds of the low fells. Stick with the main road through the hamlet (passing the masons mark to your immediate left) and follow the road to a point immediately before the steep hill. On your left here a wide gate (there's also a well hidden footpath sign to Colton Church) leads onto a rough terrace going around the hillside, marked by occasional hawthorn trees.

In a matter of yards, you'll be able to see the squat church above Colton. This is your next destination so essentially head straight towards it, this line bringing you to several kissing gates, one of which is very narrow, parcelled between two massive slabs of slate. Holy Trinity Church here at Colton serves an enormous parish area that includes both Bouth and Oxen Park as well as Colton. The little church dates from the time of Henry the Eighth and has splendid, roughly hewn rafters and beams. It also houses a bell dating from 1420 (yes....long before Henry 8) and an old font scarred by churchgoers in centuries past who used it as a whetstone to sharpen arrowheads and swords. Just outside the church is a substantial mounting block whilst one of the windows in the tower sports a Jackdaw's nest.

The walk leaves the church car parking area via a kissing gate at the top corner beyond the church hall. Follow the partially surfaced track beyond, keeping the wall to your left. At the top of the slope pass by the lone thorn tree on your right, shortly after which a rough track diverges to the right. Ignore this junction, continuing ahead to the next fork to the right, about one hundred yards later, and bear right along this. This track gradually winds downhill through an area of gorse, bracken and scrubby birch, soon entering a delightful area of Forestry Commission-owned deciduous woodland. Without doubt this track is one used over the centuries by parishioners to get from Bouth to the church; it is evidently still well used as a bridle-path between Colton and Bouth. The track winds through the woodland; go through a gate at one point and then pass a massive Scots pine before emerging from the trees at the end of a surfaced road. Walk along this, passing Old Hall Farm on your right, to reach a narrow road, turning left along which will take you back to Bouth village centre in a matter of yards.

24. Great Urswick

Route: Great Urswick – Birkrigg Common – Sunbrick – Little Urswick

Distance: 5 miles

Map: O.S.Pathfinder Sheet 635, Barrow in Furness (North).

Start: The General Burgoyne, Great Urswick. Grid Reference: SD 268744.

Access: Great Urswick is about four miles south of Ulverston. From Ulverston take the A590 towards Barrow in Furness. Some two miles out of Ulverston a minor road is signposted, left, to Great Urswick. It's not a very noticeable sign, if you cross the railway on the A590 you've gone just too far. Follow the minor road into the village, the pub is on your right just before the small housing estate.

The General Burgoyne (0229 56394)

Do you ever dream of finding a gem, a tiny pub hidden down country lanes – seemingly undiscovered by the drinking public and untouched by the passage of time (and if not, why not..)? The sort of watering hole where your great, great-grandfather would sit, draw on his clay pipe and ruminate that his great-grandfather would feel at home in the place.

The General Burgoyne is that pub.

The solid, white painted pub was built overlooking the lovely little Urswick Tarn in 1631. The builder appears to have been one "TW," he's left his initials and the date carved into one of the dark oak beams that hang low from the "lounge" ceiling. This is one of the two public rooms the pub offers. The long, thin room is lined with solid, dark old wall settles, facing each other across thick, heavy tables hewn as chunks from the living wood and roughly cut into a thin trestle shape. The centre-piece is a splendid old fireplace which seems to run for half the length of the room. Set in the wall next to it is a spice cupboard, dated to the reign of William the Third. No spices in there now, though, just the pub's resident skull. Close by is a fine array of old china/porcelain gin, brandy, sherry and rum barrels.

The smaller, bar room is similarly furnished and appointed with another massive fireplace, this one of carved wood and sporting a mirror which reflects old cider jugs and pots hung from the beams. The walls are dotted with old beer and brewery posters and labels, prints of local scenes and a selection of brasses. There's also a fruit machine, perhaps the only thing that great great grandpa wouldn't feel at home with. It's separated from the main room by the entrance passageway, dark wood panelled and decorated with the badges and plaques of a considerable number of naval vessels. Submarines. Mine host – known to one and all as Hank – served 24 years beneath the waves before chancing on Hartley's Brewery and the General.

On offer are the premium XB bitter and ordinary bitter, both on handpump, which you can also quaff on the terrace beside the pub which looks out over the tarn, a stretch of water held to be bottomless. It's also said to have drowned the original village of Urswick. The local priest, on an indeterminable date, cursed the villagers for their ungodly ways, the result being that the village sank into a suddenly-opened hole in the ground which subsequently filled with a great depth of water. This, the story goes, is why the church (worth visiting for its woodwork, the remains of a Scandinavian Cross and the Rushbearing in September) is so far away from the old part of the village. Maybe Hank should hire a mini-sub.....

The pub is named after the eponymous English General who took part in the American Civil War. He surrendered an army of 8000 to the rebels at Saratoga, New York State, in October 1777, one of the first defeats in a war that resulted in the loss of these colonies. Any such colonials chancing on the pub are enthusiastically shown "General Burgoyne's skull," for which historical artefact all financial inducements are declined by Hank, not wishing to sell off our national heritage... The General's other claim to fame is that he founded the Oaks steeplechase, one of racing's classics.

In 1991 the pub was open from 4pm-11pm on Mondays to Fridays, 12-3pm and 6pm-11pm on Saturdays and standard Sunday hours. Food is served in the evenings between 7 and 9pm, and at weekend lunchtimes. It is possible that weekday lunchtime opening may be introduced in 1992.

The Walk

(In summer, the route of this walk beyond Sunbrick hamlet is infested with high nettles and brambles – those ramblers wearing shorts beware!)

Turn left from the General Burgoyne and walk along to the junction in front of the Derby Arms, here turning right. The Derby is another Hartley's house and is open on weekday lunchtimes between noon and 2pm. Walk along this lane, essentially the village's other street, which is lined with old cottages and houses dating back to the 1600's. The village's history is a lot older, the name is Old Norse for "Village of Wild Cattle." Towards the end of the street look for the large pebble-dashed house on your left, virtually opposite two cupressor trees which guard the gate to the garden of the property opposite. Immediately beyond this pebble-dashed house a rough lane climbs up the hillside, passing between the house and a smaller building.

Follow this lane as it winds up between limestone walls capped with thorn hedges. After a while the hedges disappear. Look to your left at this point for distant views to the isolated mass of Black Combe, one of the Lake District's least known or climbed mountains. Looking back down the lane you get a good view down the shallow valleys of Lower Furness to the sea beyond the long, curving spit that is Walney Island.

At the top of the track go through the left one of the two gates and walk ahead along the line of broken walling. To your left the hilltop is capped by a large area of exposed limestone blocks, known locally as Skelmore Heads. It's the site of a British Hill Fort and there are the remains of a barrow, although not much can be seen by the untrained eye. From this modest hilltop are extensive views to the peaks of the southern Lakes, the great Forest of Grizedale and across Morecambe Bay to the Pennines and Ingleborough. Join the line of the wall which runs along below and to the east of the Fort, keeping this wall to your right. Go through the gate at the far end, near which is a waymark arrow, and walk on through the pasture, a barbed wire fence on your right. Go through the snicket stile at the end on your right and, within a few yards, a further one on your left. Walk along the left edge of two further fields and then down a short walled track to reach a junction of minor roads. Turn right, following the sign for Bardsea.

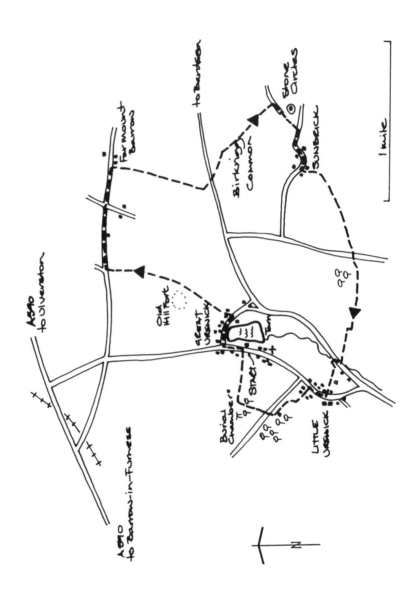

Walk along this quiet backroad for somewhat over half a mile, going straight over the crossroads and continuing towards Bardsea. The hedgerows hereabouts groan under the weight of honeysuckle, the verges are rich in Red campion, yellow Bird's foot trefoil and climbing blue Tufted vetch.

Just over the crest of a hill and immediately before the bungalow on your right take the somewhat overgrown bridleway which runs up alongside the garden wall of the bungalow. Remain with this for nearly a mile, soon passing by a hangar of beech and sycamore, after which the bridleway becomes a wide green swathe between limestone walls. Off to the left is a monument atop a hillside above Bardsea whilst ahead the bracken covered, rounded hilltop is Birkrigg Common.

Go through the ramshackle kissing gate at the end and take the left hand track gradually uphill. Go round the end of the wall and take the path which angles half-right up through the bracken (i.e. not the one which parallels the wall). Cross diagonally over the road and continue up the rutted track beyond for a short distance, then bear right along the distinct path which cuts up through the bracken. You're gradually gaining height on Birkrigg Common but all the time remaining a good distance below and to the left (east) of the summit. Join a wider path which comes in from your right and walk along to the small area of close-cropped grass. Cross this and take the widest path opposite. In a short while the delightful little village of Bardsea comes into view, nestling by a small headland jutting out into the bay.

You'll soon reach the corner of a wall; carry on with this wall off to your left, slowly loosing some height and heading, in line of sight, for Heysham Power Station, some fifteen miles away across the sands of Morecambe Bay. In a few hundred yards turn right along the rutted old cart track which comes onto the common through a gate off to your left. After just a few yards angle off to the left along one of the paths through the bracken and you'll shortly reach a fine survival of a stone circle known as the Druids' Circle. There are in fact two circles, the stones of the outermost one are lying flat and hidden in the bracken; this inner circle has ten stones and when excavated early this century produced evidence of several cremations and an urn.

The Druids' Circle on Birkrigg Common overlooks Morecambe Bay

From the circle are extensive views across the limestone belt which forms much of Furness and up across Grizedale Forest to the Fairfield Horseshoe, Helvellyn and the peaks above Coniston. Much closer to hand, the tiny island just off Bardsea is Chapel Island, site of the ruins of a medieval chapel or Cell. Take a sighting south west to the few buildings at Sunbrick hamlet and walk towards them, soon joining a minor road which leads to this tiny farming community. Most of the few cottages and farms date back several centuries, the first farm you pass, for example, has a datestone displaying 1655 to the world.

Where the road bends sharply right go straight ahead along the lane with the "no through road" sign. Go through the farmyard at the end and swing left after the barn, going through the enormous metal gate and along the rough track beyond. Stick with this track as it winds along between walls and hedges, passing through any gates which happen to be across it. Off to the left is a small old limestone quarry with a considerable lime kiln alongside it. The track gradually narrows to become a narrow path lined by a high thorn hedge with, in summer, head-high nettles and thistles. Views ahead and to the left stretch across the southern end of Walney Island to the gas platforms out in Morecambe Bay.

At the end of the path go straight across the road and through the gap stile to the left of the field gate, then walk through the boulder-strewn field to the two darker stones which take the eye ahead. These turn out to be two old stone cattle troughs. Off to your right is an area of extraordinarily twisted and gnarled old hawthorns growing on an area of exposed limestone which has been recognised as the site of a neolithic settlement. Your route lies along the left edge of the field; pass by the old kissing gate beside the short stretch of wall and walk with the hedge/wall on your left. At the far end of this field find the kissing gate through the threadbare hedge (about 20 yards into the field) and then walk down across the subsequent field towards the brown coloured cottage in the middle distance. The village ahead of you is Little Urswick, off to the right Great Urswick nestles along the north and east banks of the tarn and, on the far northern horizon, is the sharp peak of Coniston Old Man.

At the foot of the field go through the gap stile, turn right to the kissing gate, go through this and turn left, then walking alongside the wall to the lane at the bottom. Turn right along this and walk to the public footpath sign for Little Urswick, on your left about fifty yards along. Cross the stream and look to the left for a rusty red kissing gate. Once through this keep to the wall/hedge on your right and walk up along the long, narrow pasture, passing by a ruined barn some yards to your left. At the top of the pasture go through the kissing gate and walk up through the farmyard to Little Urswick's village street, turning right along this. Almost opposite you is The Swan Inn, once a farmhouse but now another of Hartley's pubs.

In about 150 yards look on your left for a public footpath sign for Dimple Holes Lane and go along this between the new houses and the old cottages. Go through the gate and carry on up past the garden, following the field road up the rough pasture. Towards the top of this field is a waymark arrow on a post, follow the direction this indicates to the far corner of the wall and then round this corner and walk to the ladder stile at the far end of the field. Beyond this is a small pasture which is home, at the time of writing, to a large number of peacocks, peahens and peachicks.

A field road curves right down the pasture, walk down this to the small stone building at the bottom end, to the left of which is a stile to climb giving access beneath a few trees and over another stile to a minor road. Go straight over this and into the field opposite, walking towards the knoll of limestone ahead. The stile out of this field is about 35 yards in from the right hand hedge, at the end of a short stretch of stone walling. Once over this climb onto the small knoll. To your left is the remains of an old chambered tomb, a limestone block perched on two others.

Walk up alongside the wall on the right of the knoll and go through the field gate at the top, turning right to follow the hedge along the bottom end of the pasture, at the top end of which is a bungalow. Climb the ladder stile and continue ahead to the gap stile, beyond which a track winds across a field littered with limestone blocks, birch and ash trees. At the far side join the old lane which soon runs past a few cottages and issues onto Great Urswick's main street. Turn right to return to the pub.

25. Broughton In Furness

Route: Broughton – Pickthall Ground – Hovel Knot – Broughton Mills

Distance: 7 Miles

Map: O.S. Pathfinder Sheet 626 Broughton in Furness & Newby Bridge and Outdoor Leisure Sheet 6, The English Lakes SW.

Start: The Square, Broughton in Furness. Grid Reference: SD 213875.

Access: Broughton is in the south western corner of Cumbria on the A595 road, about 27 miles west of Kendal and about 12 miles north of Barrow in Furness. Park in the Square or at the roadside.

The Manor Arms (0229 716286)

The end houses of one of the tall, imposing terraces that form the sides of the town square were first developed as this warm, welcoming pub more than two centuries ago. Large bow windows give views across the cobbles to the obelisk (erected to celebrate the Golden Jubilee of George 3 in 1810) and the town stocks which are the centre-point of the tree-shaded old Market Square. The one massive, high-ceilinged room is partially split into two distinct areas; on your right as you enter is the local's section, linoleum and slate floored with walls decorated by old photographs of years gone by in the town, including prints of the long-closed railway. The "lounge" section is carpeted and overlooked by umpteen prints of hunting dogs, brasses and copper oddments.

Both sections are kept at roasting temperature during the winter by open log fires, the one next to the bar is particularly cavernous. The bar itself hosts a beer festival in miniature; invariably there are three or four bitters on handpump with another two or three settling in the cellar. In early November 1991, for example, the choice was Cains Bitter, Theakstons Best, Robinsons Best and Yates, with Oak Bitter and Taylor's Landlord waiting in the wings. You can get bar snacks at virtually any time the pub is open, including splendid home made soups and broths. Opening hours tend to be about 3pm-11pm, all day on Fridays and Saturdays and possibly earlier on Tuesdays (Market Day).

Broughton in Furness

The town itself is a huddle of Elizabethan, Georgian and Victorian buildings clinging to the wooded snout of a ridge of land separating the rivers Lickle and Kirkby Pool and looking directly out over the great sandbanks that form the sweeping Duddon Estuary to the south. To the north the craggy, sharp profiled Dunnerdale Fells mark the final flourish of the mountains of the Lake District (not to forget lonely Black Combe, that isolated, brooding mass that rises to 2000 feet a few miles west of the town). The slate, whitewashed or rendered three storey houses which stride up the hillside give the village – for it is little more than such – an august, slightly aloof air, one largely as yet to be fully discovered or appreciated by the majority of visitors to Cumbria.

The Saxon name – Broughton translates roughly as an "enclosure beside a river" – evidences its long history. The church, alone on a terrace above the marshes, was founded by these Saxons; Broughton Tower, visible from the walk, was originally a Pele Tower built in the 1300's (it's now a special school) and the market charter, a sign of its historical importance, was granted in 1575, the market being established in 1539 by the Earl of Derby. Tradition has it that each year on Lammas Day, August 1st, the anniversary of this charter is celebrated by proclamation and by the throwing of coins onto the cobbles of the Market Square, such coins then scrambled for by local children.

The old stocks in the Market Square still, apparently, work but the adjoining fish slabs (where fresh sea fish and salmon used to be sold as the centre-piece of the produce market) no longer perform that particular function. Nor does the old Buttermarket retain its *raison d'être*, this belfry-capped building along the south of the Square now hosts a motorcycle museum. Tuesday is market day, the bustling livestock market cluttering up the whole town; the autumn sheep fairs, when the flocks which have close-cropped the upland pastures and fellsides during the summer are sold on, are renowned. Branwell Bronte, brother of the literary sisters, spent a short period as a private tutor in the town before embarking on his own erudite ventures.

The Walk

Commencing in the square take the road signposted for Coniston, New Street, and walk uphill out of the village. About fifty yards beyond the right hand bend take the signposted footpath on the right (just beyond the end of the estate wall) and walk along the long pasture. Without ascending it, follow the hillside around, in a couple of hundred yards passing immediately to the right of a reedy pond to reach a boundary fence. Climb the unusual metal stile here and turn left, pausing to look right to catch a glimpse of Broughton Tower, the parkland to which you've been walking through (you get a far better view of the Tower near the end of the walk).

Keep the fence to your left and curve along the old driveway towards the entrance gates. About fifty yards before reaching these cut to your right up the field and walk up the length of it, a wood-capped hill to your right. The line of oaks up this field marks the course of a narrow brook, cross this and continue to the very far left corner where a wooden stile leads over the boundary wall and onto a minor road. Go straight over the road and through the gap stile beside the field gate. Walk roughly in the direction of the public footpath sign here which points towards the first of a line of stiles, taking you towards the low, looming fells. Views from here are very pretty on a sunny autumn day, the craggy hills dappled myriad shades of ochre and gold, dotted here and there by whitewashed cottages and farmhouses and caressed by autumnally tinted woodland of gnarled old oak, rowan and beech.

The line of (wooden and gap) stiles brings you to a surfaced road some yards uphill from a group of barns and the farmhouse at Hagg. Cross straight over this road, ford the beck and go through the field gate beyond, skirting the top end of the field to find a further stile at the far side. Once through this (or the gap beside it) follow the path beneath the trees, bearing slightly left in a short distance and following what is virtually a stream bed down to the pasture beyond the trees (there's a house set higher up the bank to your right, you **don't** want the path which leads to a stile into it's lower garden). Follow the broken line of holly, thorn and beech hedge on your left, climb the solid wooden stile and continue along the narrow sunken pathway beyond.

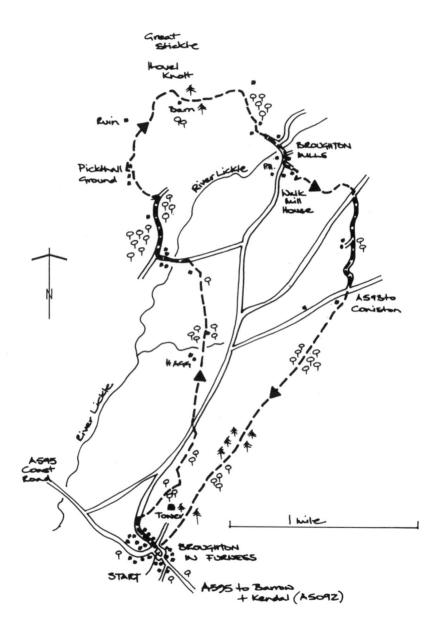

Once past the spring, the path becomes more obvious, gradually losing height but remaining some yards above the wall. At the far end of this field pass to the left of the large tree and head virtually towards the white farmhouse in the middle distance. Look for the ivy-covered old tree at the far side of the field, beside the bole of which a small gap stile gives access to a walled pathway. This acts as a stream bed for a good distance but persevere, the water eventually flows away left leaving a drier section of pathway to follow to the minor road. Turn left down this and follow it over the bridge across the Lickle, thence twisting through the settlement of barns, cottages and a milking parlour.

At the junction, bear right and walk up along the steepening, surfaced roadway which borders woodland. Pass below the cottage, some way up to your left, and continue uphill to the next junction, just beyond the bridge over a side stream. Turn left here, go through the gate and follow the field road up to the farm on the hillside, Pickthall Ground. The right of way here is very ambiguous, the map is of little help, and there is a dearth of waymarkers or footpath signs. The route I suggest is to walk up past the cottage with the yellow-painted shutters and then turn into the yard behind it. Within yards bear right and pass by the outhouse to your right. Go through the gate into the rough pasture and then follow the rutted field road gently uphill, parallelling the wall to your left. Pass the crest of the tiny crag on your right and then bear right and follow this rutted track down the pasture to a field gate (n.b. if you're heading towards the ruined barns you've missed the right turn and are on the wrong rutted track).

Go through this gate and the following one, then walk along with the wall to your right. You're heading for Hovel Knott and Great Stickle, just two of the many crags that these Dunnerdale Fells feature, the result of past volcanic activity – indeed, from certain angles some of the pikes, haws and knotts in the area seem to resemble the perfect, symmetrical volcanic cone. The track soon becomes walled on both sides, simply walk along this section and go through the gate at the far end. Turn right and follow the wide path around the foot of the Knott to reach a further gate about 200 yards further on your right, then going through this.

Stay with the track as it winds some yards above the isolated stone barn, sheltered by a number of Scots pines. The sweeping views down past these trees encompass the wide estuary of the Duddon. You should be able to pick out the submarine "pens" at Barrow in Furness and the squat tower of Millom's church rising from the flat estuary-side pastures, overshadowed by the mass of Black Combe. On the far horizon the box-like building is the nuclear power station at Heysham. Off to your left (east) is the long fellside leading up to and along the western shore of Coniston Water – Burney, Blawith Knott and Woodland Fell. Beyond this ridge and in the far distance the tops of the Pennines may be visible on a clear day, over forty miles away.

The crags of the Dunnerdale fells are the result of ancient volcanic activity

This old, walled greenway cuts around the side of the hill, gradually loosing height as the valley of the Lickle again comes into view. The scattered hamlet in the wooded valley bottom is Broughton Mills, renowned for the copious wild daffodils in bloom in early spring. To reach this stay with the track until it reaches, of all things, a picnic table and benches incongruously set in the rough pasture (presumably by the local farmer). Bear right at this juncture and walk to the gate giving access to the edge of the woods.

Follow this path down past the woods and the cottage beyond, then bear left at the entrance to the farm and follow this surfaced backroad to the hump-backed bridge over the Lickle at Broughton Mills. Presumably at one time there were several mills taking advantage of the lively river here; none now survive intact, but the house immediately downstream of the bridge has some of the trappings of an old mill.

Cross the bridge and bend right with the road a few yards further on. The route of the walk is to the left opposite the wooden village hall, up the rough driveway to Walk Mill House. Don't miss the opportunity, however, to continue up the "main" road a further fifty yards or so to reach The Blacksmiths Arms pub. This tiny place is a remarkable survival of a long gone era of the rural ale-house. I don't recommend it for the beer (keg Theakstons and Murphy's) but for the fittings and atmosphere.

Two tiny, wood panelled rooms lead off a low central passageway, the one on the left dominated by a single, huge wooden table and a wonderful old blackened range filling virtually the whole of one wall. In winter the fire is lit and you half expect a ghostly form to make use of the warming ovens and spice cupboards. Small, mullioned windows let in just enough light to ensure that old world shadows of times past still feel at home here. The other room hosts the tiny bar, further window seats and another warming fire. As if completing the scene, there's an early "VR" postbox in the wall of the pub. Opening hours seem somewhat ephemeral, but don't miss it if you get the chance.

Walk all the way up the lane and round to the left of Walk Mill House then walk along the grass strip behind the house – you're walking through the back garden and past the back door, but this is the public footpath. Within a few yards a waymarked post directs you left, up the garden and through the area of bushes to join the course of a brook. Follow this brook which will take you around the outside of the top fence of the upper garden. As the copse of trees fades away on your left, turn right and walk up the steep field to the gate some forty or so yards from the left hand corner.

Pass through this and continue uphill to a kissing gate, once through which walk on with the hedge on your left. At the top corner go through the wooden gate and bear left to the field corner. Go over the stone step stile here, turn right and walk up to the minor road. The views from here are excellent. North and west are the crinkled tops of Dunnerdale, culminating in the fell called Caw (1735 feet), east the ridge leading gradually up to Coniston Old Man and south Black Combe and the promise of the sea.

Turn right along the road and within yards fork left at the junction and walk down this minor road. At the point this bends right to enter the farmyard bear left along the muddy track and go through the gate. Beyond this the track is, surprisingly, tarred. Simply stick with this gated by-way and follow it to the main road. Cross straight over this and follow the driveway up to the isolated house, marked on an old map as the local school. Immediately before reaching it a home-made, white, directional arrow points you left, further arrows take you around the edge of the garden to a stone step stile at the far side. Go through this and continue along the rough pasture beyond, keeping the wall on your left.

Once through the very narrow gap stile at the pasture's end the path is not easy to discern. The best bet is to follow the sheep track just inside the trees on your left which emerges into another gorsey pasture. Walk in the direction of the telegraph pole you can see in the distance, the line of an old wall/hedge gradually becoming obvious to your right. Stay on this line, pass by the pole (which is virtually in the wall) and then aim ahead for the plantation of fir trees.

Down to your left is the wide mossland of Kirkby Pool, criss-crossed by drainage ditches and dotted with tiny crags and areas of scrubby woodland. Climb the wooden stile and walk through the marshy pasture to reach a gap stile beside the hedge, then following this hedge (on your left) to the corner of the woods.

Pause at this corner for a final glimpse back to Caw and the higher Dunnerdale Fells before going through the turnstile(!) gate and down the green path through the woods, a part of the Broughton Tower Estate. Ford the small stream, go through the gate at the bottom and continue along the pasture, the trees on your right. Once through the gate-sized gap at the far end favour your left hand and walk along the outside edge of the deciduous woodland. Cross the wooden stile; in a hundred or so yards the woods fold away left, downhill, at which point continue ahead in a line (keeping the few old oaks up to your right) which will take you to the tall pine tree (guarded by a sheep/deer proof cage) at the foot of the slope. From here sight Broughton Tower and aim for the tall fir trees to the left of it. This direction brings you to a sunken pathway, virtually a dry moat around the Tower's garden.

Keep this on your right and walk around this boundary, soon reaching the tall wall of the walled kitchen garden. At the far end of this another of the unusual turnstile gates leads to a path, beyond which is the football pitch and children's play area. Follow the path alongside, go through the gate at the end and walk through to the square in Broughton.

Evening on the Duddon Estuary